To Marco e Niccolò

COLLABORATION ON TEXTS
Pedro Di Vito

TRANSLATION
Claire Sapone

PAGE FORMAT
Francesco Beringi

PHOTOGRAPHS
Alfredo Palmieri
Capture Dreams Studio - Scandicci (Fi)
Archivio Giunti

The publisher will settle any reproduction rights for images
for which it has been impossible to determine the source.

www.giunti.it

Reprint					Year			
4	3	2	1	0	2008	2007	2006	2005

Printed at Giunti Industrie Grafiche S.p.A. - Stabilimento di Prato

ELISABETTA PIAZZESI

TUSCAN
DESSERTS
PASTRIES, CAKES AND SWEETS

ALL OF THE RECIPES

INTRODUCTION

Within the pages of this book I've tried to show the spontanety and cheerfulness of an affectionate gesture.

Transcribing old recipes and finding others (mostly in dusty old books) have allowed me to embrace old memories and sensations that have always been in the back of my mind. For me, cooking has forever been a natural and spontaneous part of life. It's a link between country and the nature that inhabits it. Every time I use a pan or pot in my restaurant, these ties are renewed.

While traveling the Tuscan countryside researching old and traditional (fortunately not forgotten) desserts I solidified my attachment to the earth even more. As the list of recipes grew, many of the memories I thought long forgotten returned and reminded me of the smells, aromas and emotions that forged them.

Trying out the recipes to make them 'current', I rediscovered the simple harmony of those desserts. It all came alive while my hands were covered in flour and sugar and the perfume of anise and cloves invaded my kitchen. This Tuscan harmony and the perfection of taste dates back to long ago 1533 when Catherine de' Medici introduced desserts, elixirs, jams and small pastries – often made by her – to the French nobility. Thcy were enthralled by these sweets that were made using typical Tuscan recipes and ingredients and were simple in execution.

Love and joy are the ingredients that I haven't mentioned. They're always present in these recipes. Oftentimes they're made for village festivities and religious occasions. Tuscans have always, even in moments of poverty or lacking in means, offered sweets, elixir, pastries and candies to forget, at least for a while, their problems.

It's with this philosophy of life and simplicity that this collection of recipes should be read and, I hope, used! Making sweets is an act of love toward others. It's like saying, "Hey! I was thinking of you!"

PRESENTATION

I was born on November 2nd, 1954, which I'm certain was a typical sunny autumn day: yellow and red leaves, a desperately beautiful indigo sky... the air perfumed with a mixture of wet earth and grass. I spent the first years of my life drinking in country life experiencing the marvels of childhood: discovering that rabbits are born with long tails! This I learned while grabbing one. The tail  remained in my hand but its owner escaped quickly and happily away! For several years my only friends were the fields, the cows and the fruit trees that I regularly haunted with my one friend (whose name I regret to say is lost to me). Our faces were never without the 'dirt' of homemade blackberry jam. Our ears were filled with the singing of the farmer-women at dusk. And, that aluminum can of 'Bertolini' baking powder that I used to keep my most treasured effects: berries, pebbles, sour pears and an infinite collection of dried flowers. Then, the jump to the city: sounds, colors and smells... everything was different. Sinking myself into literature and reading everything that I could get my hands on was simple, and almost a natural sequence to my earlier years. During high school, in the exact time of student political movements, I associated engaging myself with politics as being social. I won literary contests by writing about what was most amusing in reality or fantastic to me: stories, people and places. One of my favorite and fondest memories is winning a prize from the 'Fiorino d'oro' (golden florin) at Palazzo Vecchio, awarded to me by an aeronautical general. What made this so special was that the theme of my paper was about my father's memories of war.

It was during this period that I fell madly in love with Klimt, one of the greatest artists of the early 20th century.

My love blossomed during one of many trips abroad and my curiosity about everything flew from one thing to another: art, languages… to cooking. I was in Vienna, Austria (losing myself in Klimt's art) where while trying to escape from those hated Knodel (bread dumplings) I often went to hide in that fantastic Konditorei (patisserie) near the Albertina that is Demel's - one of the most famous pastry shops in the world. I already felt compelled to explore not just museums but open food markets and felt the same emotions I felt when admiring a work of art: smells, fragrances, colors, new tastes and inspiration. In Istanbul I lost myself in the spice market; fascinated and bewitched by those intense fragrances. In Darmstadt I was enchanted in front of thousands of types of cured meats and sausages. In Greece I was seduced by the charm of dining under arbors while savoring dishes with ancient names such as 'mussaka' or 'dolmades'… In the grand country of France I stood mesmerized in front of cheese carts and memorized every gesture of great chefs I saw in those enormous kitchens filled with copper cooking pots. Who knows if this was the moment the destiny of my life's work would be sealed. It was during my 16th year that I started experimenting with cooking. I enjoyed going to the market of San Lorenzo as much as going to a party with friends. My first experiments are best forgotten…when I meet some young future chef who wants to demonstrate his culinary expertise, it all comes to the forefront. Then came university and from classic Italian literature I dedicated myself entirely to cookbooks and the study of cuisine. I diligently wrote in a special notebook recipes handed down by grandmothers and noted all that was curious or significant about other peoples, cooking techniques. As the years passed I perfected and deepened my knowledge of food and came to the wonderful realization that you never finish learning about this wonderful art! I have written my experiences and deepened my knowledge inside the kitchen of my restaurant, Lo Strettoio, where still today, I find solace from life! My husband has been my traveling companion and shares my deep love of all that is used to make a meal. He and our children have sampled, many times, my inventions and experiments, which have often been daring, and have escaped unscathed! I have written, with all of these years of experience and memories, a book on Florentine cuisine and several other small books on pasta, soups and savory cuisine, etc. I now dedicate this book to Tuscan desserts and include those served in my own restaurant. Above all, these recipes are for those who want to reproduce them in their own kitchens

LO STRETTOIO

The restaurant was opened about 40 years ago from a simple and direct idea: to serve typical Tuscan home-cooked dishes in a magnificent villa overlooking Florence. The name, Lo Strettoio, comes from the impressive olive press ('strettoio' in Tuscany) that dominates the main room. The ceiling is barrel-vaulted, the walls are stone and more than two meters thick. This was the perfect environment to store produce and keep it jealously guarded from the cold of winter and the heat of summer. Inside the entrance of the locale are two rooms, one large and one small. The smaller room is used for private dining and still holds the feeding trough for the cow that turned the millstones. My husband, an expert sommelier, uses this room for tasting and jealously keeps it as a shrine to a precious collection of grappa liqueurs. Tables are set elegantly with silver and crystal as in a private home. And, from the terrace-garden the view of the city and its significant monuments is seen from a singularly new and unforgettable prospective.

HERE IS A HANDY
OVEN TEMPERATURE GUIDE:

	C° (Celcius)	F° (Fahrenheit)	Gas Mark
Very slow	120	250	1
Slow	150	300	2
Moderately slow	160	325	3
Moderate	180	350	4
Moderately hot	190	375	5
Hot	200	400	6
Very hot	230	450	7

All of the recipes are for 6-8 servings, unless stated otherwise

Some of the ingredients typically found in Tuscany may not be readily available or found near you. You can substitute some of them with similar types of foods. Of course, the flavor won't be exactly the same.

RECIPES

AFRICANI
'AFRICANI' SWEETS

◆

RECIPE FOR ABOUT 20 SWEETS: 1cup sugar, 6 egg yolks, 1/4 cup very soft butter, almond oil, candy size paper cups.

Beat the egg yolks with the sugar until pale, thick and smooth and then add the softened butter. Brush almond oil onto the paper cups (in Italian they're called 'pirottini').
Fill them with the egg mixture and place them on a baking sheet. Bake in a pre-heated 190°C/275°F oven about 15 min-utes until dark in color. These are best if served with Latte di vecchia liqueur or Limoncello.

ANICINI DI SERPIOLLE
ANISE BARS – SERPIOLLE STYLE

1 1/2 cups flour, 2 teaspoons baking powder, 1/2 cup honey (mille fiori), 2 eggs, 3/4 cup sugar, 1 teaspoon anise seeds, chopped as much as possible, butter

Sift the flour and baking powder into a large bowl. In a small saucepan melt the

honey over very low heat and cool slightly. Add it to the flour and mix it slowly with a wooden spoon.

Add the lightly beaten eggs, sugar and chopped anise seeds. Stir until completely mixed and smooth. Butter a low rectangular 15" jellyroll pan and press the dough in evenly.

Bake in a preheated 190°C/375°F oven for 20 minutes. When slightly cooled, turn out the bars and cut them into small rectangles.

These delicious, delicately flavored cookies should be eaten soon otherwise they'll loose their unique aroma.

BACI DI SERPIOLLE
COFFEE KISSES

3 cups amaretto cookie crumbs, 1 cup ladyfinger cookie crumbs, 3/4 cup butter, 1 cup sugar, 1 cup strong espresso coffee, 3 tablespoons rum, 1 cup powdered coffee (coffee that has been ground to 'super' fine like cocoa powder), 1/4 cup unsweetened cocoa powder.

Grind the amaretto cookies and ladyfingers as fine as possible and put them in a bowl. Melt the butter in a saucepan over low heat and add the sugar. As soon as the sugar has melted add the coffee and

11

the rum. Stir until the sugar is completely melted. Pour into the ground cookies and mix well until completely smooth. Cover and place the dough in the refrigerator for an hour.

Put the powdered coffee in a low dish with high borders. Using a teaspoon, form small balls with the palm of your hand and then roll them in the powdered coffee and in the cocoa. Make balls until you've finished all of the dough. Put them into candy paper cups and serve.

BACOCCOLI
RICE FRITTERS

◆

1 qt. milk, 1 cup water, 1/4 cup sugar, 1 1/2 cups rice, 2/3 cup flour, 3 teaspoons baking powder, grated peel of 1 lemon, 4 eggs, pinch of salt, oil for frying.

Bring the milk, water, sugar and salt to a boil in a large saucepan.
Add the rice and turn the flame down to low. Stirring constantly with a wooden spoon, cook the rice until all of the liquid is absorbed.
Cool slightly. While stirring, add the flour, the baking powder and lemon peel. When well mixed, set aside for one hour. Bring a pan of frying oil to a boil and drop in tablespoonfuls of batter. Drip drain and place on absorbent paper. Sprinkle with sugar.

BALLOTTE
BOILED CHESTNUTS

◆

1 1/2 lbs. chestnuts, laurel leaves, wild fennel branches.

Boil the chestnuts with several laurel

leaves and wild fennel branches for about an hour until tender when tested with a knife.
Drain when cool and peel. Served with whipped cream they're delicious!

BEFANINI
EPIPHANY OLD WITCH COOKIES

◆

3 whole eggs + 1 yolk, 2 1/2 cups flour, 1/4 cup Anisette liqueur, 1 1/4 cups sugar, 1/2 cup melted butter, 1/2 cup milk, grated rind of 1/2 an orange, 2 teaspoons baking powder.

Beat the whole eggs and sugar and then slowly add the flour and butter. Once completely blended add the Anisette liqueur, the grated rind and finally the baking powder. Flour a flat working surface and place the dough on top, cover it with a towel and let rest at least 30 minutes. Roll out the dough to about 1/4-inch. Cut-out cookies with your favorite shapes. Place on a cookie sheet and brush with the egg yolk.
Bake for about 30 minutes in a 200°C/400°F pre-heated oven. They're cooked when they become a nice brown color. These are good hot or cold.

BERLINGOZZI
ANISE TRIANGLES

◆

1 1/2 cups flour, 1 cup sugar, 4 whole eggs + 4 yolks, dash of salt, 1/8 teaspoon of anise seeds

Mound the flour onto a flat work surface and add the 4 yolks and half of the

13

sugar. Work with your hands to mix slightly and then add the rest of the eggs, sugar, pinch of salt and the anise seeds. Work the flour until you can form a ball and place in a cool, dry place for about 30 minutes. Roll out the dough to a 1/2-inch height on a floured surface and cut out small triangles. Place the triangles on a baking sheet lined with baker's paper. Bake for about 15 minutes in a preheated 190°C/375°F oven. Serve these accompanied with a nice... anise liqueur. These triangles are simpler than the 'brigidini' cookies since they don't require a special press. They're perfect for a children's party or picnic snack.

face. Cut the dough out into small pieces, flatten them with the palm of your hand and then flatten each one again with the rolling pin before placing them on a buttered and floured baking sheet. Bake for 40 minutes in a preheated 160°C/325°F oven. Remove from the baking sheet only when completely cooled. Sprinkle with the remaining sugar mixed with a little flour.

BERRICUOCCOLI
FRUIT AND NUT COOKIES

◆

1/2 cup each: finely chopped walnuts and toasted almonds, 1/4 cup finely chopped candied citron, 1/4 scant cup finely chopped candied orange, 1 1/2 cups sugar, 1/4 + 2 tablespoons honey, 2 1/4 cups flour, 2 teaspoons mixed spices: cinnamon, anise and coriander, 2 teaspoons baking powder.

Prepare the nuts and candied fruit and put them aside. Melt the honey and 1 cup of the sugar over very low heat until they become thick syrup. Mix the flour, nuts, candied fruits and spices in a large mixing bowl, then add the baking powder. Add the syrup and stir with a wooden spoon to blend all of the ingredients. Turn out onto a flat surface and knead well several moments. Cover dough and set aside for one hour. Roll out the dough to 1/4-inch on floured work sur-

BIGNÈ AL CIOCCOLATO
CHOCOLATE CREAM PUFFS

RECIPE FOR 30 BIGNÈ: 1 1/2 cups water, 1 cup flour, 1/2 cup butter, pinch of salt, 5 eggs, slightly beaten, 1 tablespoon sugar.
FOR THE CREAM FILLING: 1/3 cup sugar, 2 egg yolks, 1/4 cup sweetened cocoa powder, 1/4 cup flour, 2 cups milk, 1 vanilla bean.
FOR GARNISH: 1 1/2 oz. dark chocolate + a little milk.

Prepare the puffs: bring the water, butter and salt to a boil in a medium saucepan. Remove from heat and slowly add, stirring, the flour and sugar. Make sure to mix vigorously with a wooden spoon and so that all of the ingredients are blended well. Put the pan back over a low flame and cook until the mixture is thick and loosened from the sides of the pan and remove from heat. Add the eggs one at a time, mixing well each time. Mix well and set aside to cool for at least 10 minutes. Fill a large pastry bag (use a wide-hole straight tip) with the dough and squeeze walnut sized balls onto a buttered and floured baking sheet. Bake

15

in a 160°C/325°F pre-heated oven for 15 minutes. As soon as they come out of the oven, poke a hole into one side of each of the puffs. Cool.

Make the cream filling: Put the yolks and sugar in a saucepan and beat them until pale and smooth. Add the flour and cocoa powder, beating continuously. Add the milk, beat. Turn on the flame and put in the vanilla bean. Cook, stirring continuously with a whisk, until the cream becomes thick.

Cool. When the cream is cold, fill a pastry bag (small straight tip) and fill each of the pastry puffs. Melt the dark chocolate with a little milk if necessary in a small saucepan over simmering water.

After filling each puff, place them on a serving tray and drizzle the melted chocolate on top of each.

BISCOTTI DI POMARANCE
POMARANCE COOKIES
◆

1 cup warm milk, 3 teaspoons baking powder, 2 3/4 cups flour, 1/2 cup corn meal, 3/4 cup sugar, 1/4 cup lard, 1/4 cup softened butter, pinch of salt.

Dissolve the baking powder in the warm milk. Mix the flour and cornmeal together in a large bowl and add the milk, sugar, lard and butter.

Mix with hands until blended and turn out onto a floured surface and knead until smooth. Divide the dough into many small baguettes. Form the baguettes gently into an 'S' shape.

Set the cookies on a greased baking sheet, well spaced. Cover the cookies with a floured towel and set them aside to rise for an hour in a warm spot. Bake the cookies in a pre-heated 220°C/425°F

oven for about 20 minutes. Cool completely. Then store well in a hermetically sealed jar. They're a really excellent snack or served with a nice liqueur at the end of a meal.

BISCOTTI DI PRATO
BISCOTTI OF PRATO

4 whole eggs + 4 egg yolks, 3 1/2 cups sugar, 4 1/2 cups flour, 1 cup sweet almonds (whole), grated rind of 1 orange, 1 egg yolk, beaten slightly.

Beat the egg yolks with the sugar – using either a hand whisk or electric mixer - until they are pale, smooth and form a ribbon when dribbled from the whisk. If the dribble doesn't float on top of the yolks, you need to keep beating. While beating, slowly add the flour, the almonds, and orange peel. Beat another 5 minutes or so.

Form 2 long loaves with the dough that are about 1 1/2 inches high. Set them on a greased or papered baking sheet and set aside for 30 minutes. Brush the loaves with the beaten egg yolk.

Bake in a pre-heated 180°C/350°F oven for about 15 minutes. Be careful because this time is only an indicator... the secret to baking these correctly is in the 'eye' of the cook. Remove from oven and cut them into diagonal slices using a serrated knife. Serve cold.

The old saying goes: "I biscotti e il morellino, ti danno l'ultimo ritocchino" or rather, biscotti and morellino wine are the final touch to any meal.

The witty saying still remains correct and popular while demonstrating that simplicity is still perfect and true... just like biscotti served with wine.

BISCOTTI UBRIACHI DI MONTALCINO
MONTALCINO DRUNKEN COOKIES

◆

2 cups flour, 2 teaspoons active dry beer yeast, 4 eggs, slightly beaten, 1 cup toasted almonds, chopped, 1 1/3 cups sugar, 1 cup robust red wine (like Brunello), 2 teaspoons mixed spices: cinnamon, cloves, anise.

Put the flour and beer yeast on a flat work surface and form a crater in the center where you'll pour the eggs and 1/4 cup of the chopped nuts. Knead slightly. Put the sugar, wine and spices in a pan and bring to a boil. Boil several minutes and remove from heat to cool completely.

Begin kneading the dough again and add the wine mixture little by little until it is all used. Knead in, if necessary, more flour if the dough is too sticky. Form a ball and cover with a towel. Let rest at least an hour. Roll out the dough on a floured surface to 1/2-inch thick. Cut out rectangles and sprinkle the remaining almonds on top.

Place on a buttered and floured baking sheet and bake in a pre-heated 160°C/325°F oven for about 1 hour. Since the end result of these cookies is rather dark in color, they're nicknamed 'tegole' or roof-tiles. They're often accompanied by cold Moscadello wine.

BISCOTTONE ALLA MARMELLATA DI CILIEGE
GIANT CHERRY JAM TURNOVER

📷

1 recipe Pastry dough (Pasta Frolla, see recipe D), 1 cup cherry jam, 1 egg yolk, slightly beaten.

Prepare the pastry dough according to the recipe. When cold, roll it out into a 1/4-inch high square on a floured work surface. Spread the cherry jam onto half of the dough and fold the other half over. Pinch to seal the edges. Place the turnover on a baking sheet that has been covered with oven paper and brush the top with the beaten egg yolk. Bake in a pre-heated 200°C/400°F oven for 20 minutes. Cool and cut into small rectangles and place them on a paper-lined tray.

BOLLI DI LIVORNO
LIVORNESE COOKIE BALLS

◆

12 oz. bread dough (Pasta di pane, see recipe C), 1 cup sugar, 5 whole eggs, 1/2 cup Maraschino liqueur, 1 tablespoon olive oil, orange essence water, 1/8 teaspoon cinnamon, 1/8 teaspoon powdered anise seed, flour, 1 egg white beaten, 2 tablespoons lard.

Knead the bread dough for several minutes. Cover and set aside to rise in a dry spot for at least an hour.
Beat the eggs, slowly adding the sugar and little by little the Maraschino liqueur, olive oil, several drops of orange water and the spices. Beat well.
Kneading with your hands blend in the liquid mixture into the bread dough. Add flour as necessary to prevent the dough from getting sticky.
Form small balls and flatten them with the palm of your hand. Place them on a baking sheet that has been greased with lard and floured. Set the buns aside for 15 minutes before brushing the tops with beaten egg white.
Bake in a pre-heated 220°C/425°F oven for about 20 minutes. These should be eaten cold, served with any 'rustic' jam – such as quince apple butter.

BOMBE DI CANDITI
CANDIED FRUIT BOMBS

◆

1/4 cup butter, 1/2 cup sugar, 1 1/2 cup amaretto cookie crumbs, 1/4 cup each: candied orange and citron, 1 tablespoon chopped candied pumpkin, 1/4 cup chestnut flour, 3/4 cup Alkermes liqueur, 1/2 cup powdered sugar, candy size paper cups.
VARIATION: 1/2 cup toasted almonds.

Melt the butter and sugar in a small saucepan. Grind the amaretto cookies until fine and put them in a large bowl. Add the chopped orange, citron and pumpkin. Stir. Add the chestnut flour and wet the entire mixture with the Alkermes liqueur. Add the melted butter and sugar and mix them into the fruit and cookies. Blend with a wooden spoon until a hard sticky ball is formed. Put it in the refrigerator for an hour. Put the powdered sugar on a flat plate. With the batter form balls the size of walnuts with your hands and roll them in the powdered sugar. Put the 'bombe' into candy paper cups and refrigerate them at least 10 minutes before serving.

A frequent variation is the use of chopped toasted almonds for rolling instead of the powdered sugar.

The 'bombe' are less sugary and more appropriate for the filling.

BOMBOLONI
DONUTS

2 oz. fresh compressed active beer yeast, 2 tablespoons warm water, 2 1/2 cups flour, 1/3 cup sugar, 1/3 cup butter, softened, grated rind of 1/2 lemon, oil for frying.

Dissolve the yeast with the warm water. Mix the flour, sugar, butter, grated rind and dissolved yeast together. Knead with your hands until smooth. Let rise, covered by a cloth, in a warm place for 2 to 3 hours. Roll out the dough to 1/2-inch thick and cut out the donuts with either a cutter or a floured glass. Set the cut disks aside on a floured surface to rise another 30 minutes.

Fry the donuts in boiling oil. Drain and dry on absorbent paper. Sprinkle with sugar and serve immediately. Variation: fill the 'puffed' ones with your favorite jam or pastry cream or... for the real sweet-tooth... chocolate!

An undoubtedly rich and calorie-filled dessert – and shunned today – is slowly coming back to style. You find the signs ("Bomboloni Caldi") in the windows of the best pastry shops... at the classic time for an afternoon snack... and still hot from the fryer.

BRIGIDINI DI LAMPORECCHIO
ANISE WAFER COOKIES

◆

Recipe for about 1 pound of cookies: *2 1/4 cups flour, 3/4 cup sugar, 8 eggs, 10 drops of anise extract.*

You will need a 'brigidino' press to cook these wafers. They are available in good cooking supply shops; they're also known as wafer presses. It is more difficult to find the authentic 'printed' type with the leaf decoration in the center.

Without a press, the taste is not missing but the 'look' is.

You can also bake the 'brigidini' in the oven on bakers' paper, however. Mound the flour and sugar on a flat surface and form a crater in the center.

Crack two of the eggs into the center. Working quickly, blend the ingredients with your hands. Add two more eggs, the anise extract and blend. Continue in this manner, working continuously until all of the eggs are added and the dough is completely blended and smooth. Let rest one hour. Divide the dough into many walnut-size balls. Flatten the balls with the press and bake them over an open flame for a short while.

Or, you can flatten them, place on a baking sheet lined with baker's paper and cook them in a pre-heated 200°C/400°F oven until just golden.

These dainty bits have a curious name: perhaps born in the Convent of Santa Brigida of Lamporecchio near Pistoia. It was in 1927 that the small village was incorporated into the larger county of Pistoia. There isn't a regional festival or market in Tuscany that doesn't herald these sweets... and there is no child or adult that doesn't love them!

BRUCIATE
ROASTED CHESTNUTS

◆

This recipe has no quantities because... you can eat one after the other... especially if you're sitting in front of a fire with friends on a cold winter's night... well... you'll need a lot! You'll need a chestnut pan – the kind with the holes on the bottom. After cutting a slice into each chestnut (called castrating), place them in the pan over an open flame. Turn them often to raise their temperature so that the skins blacken. Once cooked, place them in a towel, preferably wool, to 'stew'. Peel and... have a nice time!

BRUCIATE BRIACHE
DRUNKEN CHESTNUTS

◆

1 lb. chestnuts (marron type), 1 cup 50° Grappa liqueur, 2 tablespoons sugar.

First, prepare the chestnuts by "castrating" them (cut them with a sharp knife, slashing them across the fattest part) and toast them in a chestnut pan over an open flame.

Peel the toasted chestnuts, place them in a bowl and pour in the Grappa. Set aside for an hour. Drain and put them in a pan with the sugar and heat.

Once hot, set fire to them and take them directly to the table, stirring with a wooden spoon to maintain the flame.

You can substitute the Grappa with some strong Jamaican rum for a slightly different flavor.

During winter, in the country, and better yet among friends, chestnuts prepared like this are a nice change and a good reason to enjoy them with company.

BRUTTI MA BUONI
UGLY-BUT-GOOD COOKIES

RECIPE FOR ABOUT 30: 5 egg whites, 2.2 lbs. sugar, grated rind 1 lemon, 1/2 cup peeled chopped almonds (sweet and bitter mix), 1 cup peeled hazelnuts.

Whip the egg whites to a stiff peak and then add the lemon peel. Slowly add the almonds and the sugar, mixing to a dense consistency. Butter a cookie sheet and spoon small amounts onto the sheet and set aside for 10 minutes. Bake in a preheated 160C°/325°F oven for about 30 minutes until golden in color. Just like their name, these 'crunchy mountains' are not pretty... but they're so good!

BUCCELLATO
FRUIT CAKE – LUCCA STYLE

1/2 oz. fresh compressed active beer yeast, 2 cups flour, 3/4 cups sugar, 1/4 cup melted butter, 2 eggs, beaten, 1/2 cup mixed fruit: raisins, candied peels, fresh lemon peel, 2 teaspoons anise seeds, 1 teaspoon baking soda, 1 egg white.

Prepare the yeast: dissolve the dry yeast with a little flour in half a glass of warm water and set aside to rest for 30 minutes. Mound the flour on a flat work surface and knead in the melted butter, 1/4 cup of sugar, candied fruit and raisins, beaten eggs and anise seeds. Knead vigorously, adding a little warm water while working. Add the prepared yeast and continue to knead several minutes until the dough is sooth and elastic.

Shape the dough into a ring and brush it all with the egg white, which has been mixed with the rest of the sugar. Place the dough in a buttered 8 1/2 x 4 1/2 x 2 1/2" loaf pan. (Buccellato is baked in various shapes – you can also use a ring pan or a half-moon shaped tin as well). Cut the surface in several places with a sharp knife. Set aside for 20 minutes. Bake in a pre-heated 190°C/375°F oven for 45 minutes. In a variation no longer in use, fresh rosemary was added to the dough and the top was sprinkled with more raisins and candied fruit before baking.

BUDINO DI MANDORLE
ALMOND PUDDING

◆

1 cup chopped, peeled almonds, 3/4 cup sugar, 6 egg whites.

Grind the almonds to a fine powder and set aside. Melt the sugar in a pot over low heat and make certain not to let it become too brown.

Add the almonds and cook until they become crunchy and dark colored. Set aside to cool completely. Whip the egg whites to stiff peaks and fold in the cooled almonds. Pour into a buttered pudding dish and refrigerate several hours. Serve very cold.

This dessert – known as a 'dolce di recupero' or rather 'left-overs' – was born from the need to use leftover egg whites. This dish is light and easily digested thanks to its delicate structure.

BUDINO DI MARRONI
CHESTNUT PUDDING

◆

2.2 lbs. chestnuts ('marron' type), 1 bunch wild fennel, 6 oz. dark unsweetened cocoa powder, 3/4 cup softened butter, 1 cup powdered sugar, 3 amaretto cookies, crumbled, 20 candied cherries.

Boil the chestnuts and fennel for about 1 1/2 hours, peel and puree (You can still find wild fennel in bunches at the 'fruttivendolo' – the old-fashioned fruit & vegetable store). Add the cocoa powder and sugar, mix well, then add the softened butter and amaretto cookie crumbs to the puree. Mix well with your hands until completely blended. Fill a shallow 1 1/2-quart pudding dish with some wet gauze and put the batter in so that it covers the bottom and sides well. Beat the dish on the counter to 'flatten' out the mixture. Refrigerate 2 hours, un-mold

and garnish with candied cherries.

For a special dinner: garnish with candied violets. I much prefer these garnishes to the ultramodern and ever-present whipped cream.

BUDINO DI MASCARPONE
MASCARPONE CHEESE PUDDING

10 oz. (1 3/4 cups) fresh mascarpone cheese, 4 eggs, separated, 4 tablespoons sugar, 3/4 cup Vin Santo wine, ladyfinger cookies.

Beat the egg yolks and sugar until smooth and pale in color. Add the mascarpone a little at a time and continue beating until smooth. In another bowl beat the egg whites until they form stiff peaks and fold them into the cheese mixture. Dip the ladyfingers into the Vin Santo and place them in the bottom and sides of a serving bowl. Pour the cream over the top and place it in the fridge for several hours before serving. This pudding was characteristic of Sunday luncheon. It was simple to make and, as a child, I got to make it because it didn't require cooking. Little by little Florentine families stopped making this dessert. These days I make this concoction early in the year when I can get eggs fresh from the farmer; as the antique proverb says: "Gennaio ovaio", or rather, January is a good month for chickens to produce eggs.

BUDINO DI RISO
RICE PUDDING

1 cup Arborio rice, 1 qt. milk, cup sugar, 1/2 cup raisins, softened in hot water for 10 minutes, 1 tablespoon butter, dash of salt, 2 eggs + 2 yolks, 3/4 cup Vin Santo wine, grated bread crumbs.

Cook the rice, milk and sugar in a medium sized pot for about 30 minutes. When half cooked, add the softened raisins, butter and pinch of salt.
Set aside to cool completely. Beat the eggs and the yolks, add the Vin Santo and mix well, then add them to the rice. Pour into a 2-quart capacity ring mold that has been buttered and 'floured' with breadcrumbs.
Preheat oven to 180°C/350°F and set the pudding aside to rest 10 minutes before placing in the oven.
Bake about 30 minutes or until golden. Test with a toothpick for doneness.
Un-mold while warm and serve immediately. For a delicious variation, fill the center with pastry cream.

BUDINO DI SEMOLINO
SEMOLINA PUDDING

◆

PUDDING BASE: 1 qt. milk, 1 cup sugar, 2/3 cup semolina flour, 6 egg yolks, 2 egg whites, 3 tablespoons chopped candied citron, 3 tablespoons sultana raisins, plumped in hot water then squeezed to remove excess water, 1 cup rum, butter, bread crumbs.

FOR THE CREAM: 2 egg yolks, 2 tablespoons sugar, 2 cups milk, boiled then cooled completely, pinch of salt, 1 vanilla bean.

Mix the milk and sugar together in a pot and bring to a boil; remove from heat and slowly pour in the semolina flour, mixing constantly with a wooden spoon or a whisk.
Return pot to heat and cook, stirring

constantly, for about 10 minutes. Remove from heat and cool completely. In a mixing bowl, beat the 6 yolks; set aside. In another bowl, beat the whites to form soft peaks.
Gently, fold the beaten yolks and whites into the cooled semolina. Fold in the candied citron and raisins.
Lastly, add the rum. Butter and sprinkle with bread crumbs a 2-qt. baking dish. Pour in the batter and place the baking dish into a large baking pan and fill the outer pan with hot water.
Bake in a pre-heated 220°C/425°F for 45 minutes.
Test to see if a toothpick comes out clean. Serve this dessert either hot or cold but... it is really excellent when served with a simple cream that is made this way: using a whisk, beat the egg yolks with the sugar and slowly add the flour in a small pot.
Add the cooled milk, pinch of salt and a vanilla bean.
Cook over low heat until thickened; remove the vanilla bean. Cool and serve along with the pudding.
If the pudding was cooked in a ring pan, serve it in the center.

BUDINO FARRO E BALLOTTE
SPELT WHEAT
AND CHESTNUT PUDDING

◆

2/3 cup spelt wheat, 1 cup boiled chestnuts (see recipe "Ballotte"), 4 cups milk, 1/2 cup sugar, 1/4 cup butter, 1/4 cup raisins, softened by soaking 10 minutes in hot water, 1/2 cup Limoncello liqueur (Latte di Vecchia liqueur, if available), bread crumbs, dark chocolate for garnish.

Boil the spelt wheat according to package instructions. Drain and cool slightly. Place the wheat in a medium sized pot along with the prepared chestnuts, sugar and milk.

Cook slowly over low heat, stirring continuously for about 20 minutes. Once cooked, add butter, raisins, and the Latte di Vecchia (or Limoncello). Pour mixture into a 2-qt. baking dish buttered and lightly 'floured' with the breadcrumbs. When cooled refrigerate for several hours before serving. Before bringing to the table, un-mold the pudding onto a platter and garnish with grated dark chocolate flakes.

CASTAGNE CARAMELLATE
CANDIED CHESTNUTS

◆

2 lbs. large chestnuts, 10 laurel leaves, 1 branch dried wild fennel leaves, 1 qt. milk, 1 cup sugar.

Fill a large pot with cold water, add the chestnuts, laurel and fennel leaves.
Simmer the chestnuts for about twenty minutes.
Drain, remove the leaves and peel the chestnuts. Put them in another pot with the milk and cook until they're soft.
At this point, drain and remove any excess peel.
Put the sugar and 2 tablespoons of water in a saucepan. Cook the sugar over a very low fire until it becomes lightly golden in color.
Put the chestnuts on a serving tray and pour the sugar syrup on top.
These are a delicious treat served cold with a glass of herb-flavored liqueur.

CASTAGNE SECCHE
DRIED CHESTNUTS

◆

1/2 lb. dried chestnuts, 1 cup white wine, salt, laurel leaves.

Peel the dried chestnuts and place them in a pot of cold water along with the wine, some salt and the laurel leaves. Cook, covered, for about 2 hours at moderate heat.
They're good either hot or cold, served with the water they were cooked in.

CAVALLUCCI
SIENESE CANDIED FRUIT COOKIES

FOR ROUGHLY 40 COOKIES: 2 cups water, 1 1/2 cups sugar, 1 1/2 cups flour, 1/2 cup chopped walnuts, 1/4 cup chopped candied orange peel, 1 teaspoon ground anise seed, pinch of cinnamon, 1 tablespoon honey (mille fiori), butter.

In a small saucepan, make syrup with the water and sugar by mixing and heating them over a very low flame for about 20 minutes. You'll know it's ready when you drop some into a glass of cold water and the drop floats. Slowly add the flour, walnuts, orange peel, spices and honey, mixing after each addition until blended thoroughly. Place mixture on a well-floured surface and roll it out to a height of 1/2-inch. Cut the cookies using a floured glass. Flour the cookies.

Transfer the cavallucci to a buttered cookie sheet and bake them at 160°C/325°F for about 30 minutes, being careful that they remain a very light color – not golden.

CENCI
MARDI GRAS 'RAG' COOKIES

◆

1 1/2 cup flour, 1/4 cup softened butter, 3 eggs, 4 tablespoons sugar, 1 teaspoon vanilla extract, 1 tablespoon Vin Santo wine, pinch of salt, olive oil for frying, 1 cup powdered sugar.

Mound the flour onto a flat work surface and cut the butter on top. Mix gently with your hands and add the sugar, eggs, Vin Santo and salt. Knead until smooth and elastic. Set aside, covered with a cloth, for about an hour.

Flour a flat surface and roll out the dough to about 1/4 –inch high. Using a zigzag edged roller cut the dough into large 1 x 5"-inch strips. You can either leave the strips like this or you can tie them into a knot or whatever... these are called 'cenci', which means 'rags', because they really are shaped and cut in all different ways. Fry the rags in abundant hot oil until golden. Drip well and set to dry on absorbent paper. Sprinkle liberally with powdered sugar.

CIALDE ALLE MANDORLE TOSTATE
TOASTED ALMOND WAFERS

◆

16 egg whites, 2 1/2 cups sugar, 2 1/4 cups flour, 1/2 cup melted butter, 1 cup sparkling white wine, peeled almonds.

Beat the egg whites with the sugar, flour and melted butter. When well mixed and smooth, add the white wine and mix well until blended. Pre-heat the oven to 180°C/350°F. Heat a baking sheet then butter it liberally.

Using a ladle, spoon the egg mixture onto the sheet forming 6-inch disks. You must work quickly to prevent the baking sheet from cooling.

Sprinkle the disks with the almonds and bake. Watch them carefully and remove from oven as soon as they start to become golden. Cool.

My husband loves these served with a dollop of fig jam in the center.

CIAMBELLA DI RIFREDO
RIFREDO RING CAKE

◆

2 1/4 cups flour, 1 1/4 cups sugar, 3 teaspoons active dry beer yeast, 3 eggs, 1/4 cup butter, grated peel 1 lemon, 1 egg yolk, slightly beaten.

Mound the flour, sugar and yeast on a flat work surface. Form a crater in the center and pour in the eggs, add the butter cut into small pieces and the grated lemon peel.

Knead with your hands until the dough takes on a smooth and sticky consistency. Set the dough aside, covered by a towel, for one hour. Butter and flour a 9" ring pan, tap the pan to eliminate the excess flour.

Brush the dough with the egg yolk and bake in a pre-heated 190°C/ 375°F oven for 40 minutes. Turn out when completely cooled.

This cake is excellent when sliced, dipped in milk, and served as an energetic breakfast or afternoon snack.

29

CIAMBELLONE BICOLORE
TWO-COLOR BUNDT CAKE

4 eggs, 1 1/2 cup sugar, 2 1/2 cups flour, 2 teaspoons baking powder, 1 cup olive oil, 1 cup milk, 1/2 cup powdered un-sweetened dark cocoa powder, butter, breadcrumbs.

Beat the eggs with the sugar until light and foamy.

Mix the flour and baking powder together until blended and add them all at once to the eggs.

Always beating with a whisk, add the oil and beat the dough until smooth. Lastly, add the milk and beat until smooth but while still maintaining the batter's fluffiness. Pour half of the batter into a buttered and floured with breadcrumbs 10" high-sided-ring pan.

Set aside. Add the cocoa powder to the remaining batter and mix.

Pour the chocolate batter on top of the other layer. Bake in a 190°C/375°F preheated oven for 40 minutes.

Once cooled, turn out and dust with powdered sugar.

Slice the cake and serve the slices drizzled with a light vanilla cream, for a truly delicious dessert.

CIARAMICOLA
LIQUEUR CAKE

◆

2 3/4 cups flour, 1 oz. fresh compressed active beer yeast, pinch of salt, 2 eggs, beaten slightly, 1 1/4 cups sugar, 1 teaspoon vanilla extract, grated rind 1 lemon, 2 tablespoons softened butter, 1/2 cup Alkermes liqueur, 1/2 cup Anisette liqueur (Mistrà).
TOPPING: 2 egg whites, 1/2 cup sugar

Mix 1/4 cup of the flour with a pinch of salt and the yeast dissolved in warm water. Cover with a cloth and set aside for 30 minutes to rise. Pour the remaining flour onto a flat work surface and pour the prepared yeast on top.
Add the 2 beaten eggs, sugar, vanilla and lemon peel. Knead for about 10 minutes, adding the Alkermes and Anisette liqueurs a little at a time. Form the dough into a ball and set aside, covered, for an hour. Butter and flour a shallow 8" ring baking pan and fill it with the dough. For the topping: beat the egg whites with the sugar until foamy. Brush the top of the dough. Bake the bread for 30 minutes in a pre-heated 190°C/375°F oven. Turn out of pan only when completely cold.

COMPOSTA DI CREMA ALLA MODA DI PRATO
CANDIED CHESTNUT COMPOTE

◆

1 cup 'marron glacee' candied chestnuts, 2 cups Alkermes liqueur, 4 egg yolks, 4 tablespoons sugar, 1 cup milk, 1/8 cup flour, 1 vanilla bean, 1/4 cup peeled sliced almonds.

Boil the milk and set it aside to cool. Put the candied chestnuts into a bowl

with the Alkermes and let them marinate for at least an hour.
Prepare the cream by putting the following into a large saucepan: yolks, sugar and flour. Whisk together and slowly add the cooled milk. Add the vanilla bean and cook the mixture over low heat, stirring constantly with a wooden spoon.
Once the cream begins to boil, continue cooking and stirring 5 more minutes. Remove from heat and remove the vanilla bean. Drain the chestnuts, dry them with a paper towel and put two into the bottom of each dessert cup.
Pour the cream over the top and place them in the refrigerator for at least 2 hours. Toast the almonds in the oven for 3-4 minutes and put them on top of the compote before serving.
For a nice variation: instead of almonds, drizzle each dessert with hot melted chocolate before serving.

CONSERVA DI UVA NERA
BLACK WINE GRAPE JELLY

◆

QUANTITY FOR 4 1/2-CUP JARS: 6-7 lbs. black wine grapes (sangiovese), 1/2 cup candied citron, 1/4 cup + 1 tablespoon dried mustard, 1/4 cup sugar.

Carefully de-stem the grapes and wash them. Squash them using a food mill over a large pot (preferably ceramic) so that you get all of the liquid (called wine must). Add the sugar and cook over a very low flame for 2 to 2 1/2 hours, stirring often, until the liquid becomes very thick. Remove from heat and add the candied citron and the mustard. You may want to sift the mustard in to prevent it from forming lumps. Cool and then pour the spicy jelly into jars that have a hermetic seal. Seal in hot water bath if preserving. This jelly is wonderful as an accompaniment to boiled meats or meatloaf (which is usually so drab) and gives them an added zing.

CONSERVA DI ZUCCA
PUMPKIN PRESERVE

◆

QUANTITY FOR 4 1/2-CUP JARS: 6-7 lbs. Pumpkin, 2.2 lbs. sugar (more or less, as it should be the same amount as the prepared puree).

32

Wash the pumpkin, peel it and chop it into large pieces and place them into a large pot of water.
Boil for just a few minutes and, once well drained, puree. Put the puree into another large pot and add the sugar – make sure that the sugar is the same quantity as the puree.
Cook over a low flame, stirring often with a wooden spoon, for about an hour until the consistency is thick and smooth. Pour into prepared canning jars. This preserve is wonderful as an accompaniment to roasted or boiled meats. If not using within one month, hot water seal is necessary.
To successfully prepare this preserve it is indispensable that the pumpkin you use be in season with a firm, juicy pulp. The best type to use is the 'Muscade' pumpkin that has an orange-red peel, is round, deep-ribbed and smooth.

COPATE SENESI
SIENESE NOUGAT ROUNDS

◆

2 cups honey (mille fiori), 2 1/2 cups sugar, 1 cup Vin Santo wine, 1 1/2 cups peeled and toasted almonds, chopped finely, edible pastry paper.

Melt the honey, sugar and Vin Santo in a saucepan and cook over a low flame, stirring only by turning the pot, until caramelized. Add the almonds and stir with a wooden spoon. Place over the low flame again and cook for several more minutes, stirring constantly. Remove from heat but keep the saucepan near the burners so that the mixture remains warm and doesn't solidify. Working quickly with wet hands, form the nougat into a long cylinder that's 1 1/2-inches thick. Place the cylinder on a flat surface – preferably marble if available – and slice off pieces that are about 1/8 cup in size. Place the edible pastry paper on your work surface and place each piece in the center. Top them with more paper. Press down gently with the palm of your hand. They're ready: the best place to store 'copate' so that they remain fresh and fragrant is to place them in a cool, dry place.

COROLLI DI SIENA
SIENESE COROLLO COOKIES

1 oz. fresh compressed active beer yeast, 2 1/2 cups flour, 1 egg, 1/2 cup sugar, 1/4 cup honey (mille fiori), 1/2 cup (scant) oil, 1/8 cup anise seeds.

Dissolve the yeast with several tablespoon of tepid water. Mound the flour on a flat surface and form a crater in the center. Fill the crater with the egg, sugar, honey, oil and the prepared yeast. Mix quickly

and knead until the dough is elastic and smooth. Cover it with a cloth and set aside to rise for two hours. Divide the dough into small fist-sized mounds (about 1/4 cup). Form donuts with the mounds and set them on a baking sheet lined with oven paper. Sprinkle the tops with the anise seeds. Bake in a pre-heated 190°C/375°F oven for 30 minutes. These cookies store extremely well and would last a long time, however, if you eat them accompanied by some Vin Santo... maybe not! In some places around Siena, these sweets are glazed with white frosting.

CRESCENTINE
CRESCENT TREATS

◆

11/2 cups flour, 2 teaspoons active dry beer yeast, pinch of salt, 1 tablespoon oil, 1 tablespoon lard, 1/2 cup milk, oil for frying, 1/2 cup sugar.

On a flat work surface mix the flour, yeast and salt with your hands. Add the oil, lard and the half-cup of milk. Knead well with floured hands. Form a ball with the dough, cover and set aside for about 45 minutes. Fill a pan with frying oil and bring it to a boil. While the oil is heating, roll out the dough on a well-floured surface to a height of 1/4-inch. Using a zigzag rolling-cutter cut out diamond shapes.

Drip the diamonds into the hot oil and cook until just golden on both sides. Drain and dry on absorbent paper and sprinkle with sugar. Should be served while still hot.

CROSTINI DOLCI
BREAD CAKES

6 slices day-old Italian bread, 1 cup milk, warmed, 1 tablespoon vanilla sugar (or add regular sugar + 1/2 teaspoon vanilla extract), 2 eggs, 1/2 cup breadcrumbs, 1/2 cup flour, oil for frying.

APRICOT SYRUP: *2 cups water, 1 lb. ripe apricots, 1 cup sugar, 1 lemon.*

MIXED FRUIT COMPOTE: *1 cup water, 1/2 lemon, 1 Williams pear, washed, peeled, cored, 1 Golden Delicious apple, washed, peeled, cored, 1/2 cup dried apricots, 1/4 cup dried pitted prunes.*

Prepare the Crostoni: put the sugar in a mixing bowl with the warm milk and mix. Slice the bread into slices that aren't too thin or too thick. Put the slices into the milk. Put the yolks into a shallow bowl and beat slightly. Prepare one plate with the flour and another with the breadcrumbs.

Dredge the bread first with the flour, then dipped in the eggs then dredge again with the breadcrumbs.

Fry the bread slices in abundant hot oil until golden. Dry them on absorbent paper. Put the cooked slices on a tray with a bowl of the apricot syrup and a bowl of the mixed fruit compote. Prepare the Apricot Syrup: wash, pit and chop into pieces the apricots.

Put them in a saucepan with the sugar, water and lemon juice. Cook for 30 minutes, stirring often until the syrup is thickened. Strain to remove pieces. Set aside to cool. Prepare the Mixed Fruit Compote: Plump the dried apricots and prunes in hot water for 10 minutes. In the meantime, put the water and grated peel of half of a lemon in a saucepan. Add the chopped pear, apple, and plumped fruits. Cook to boiling and boil one minute. Cool and serve with any remaining water drained.

DIOSPERI AL VINO BIANCO
PERSIMMONS WITH WHITE WINE AND RICOTTA CHEESE

◆

4 large, ripe persimmons, 4 tablespoons sugar, 1/2 cup white wine, 2 cups fresh ricotta or raveggiolo cheese.

Wash the persimmons (called 'diosperi' in Tuscany) and dry them. Gently remove the stem, cut them in half horizontally and remove just a bit of the pulp with a teaspoon. Mix the ricotta (or raveggiolo) cheese with the wine and sugar in a bowl. Fill a pastry bag with the filling and squeeze it into the center of the prepared persimmons. Refrigerate. These are good as an after dinner dessert but just as tasty as an afternoon snack.

DOLCE DI FARRO
SPELT WHEAT DESSERT

◆

3/4 cup spelt wheat, 1 qt. milk, 1/2 scant cup sugar, 1/2 cup chopped peeled almonds, 1/2 cup chopped candied citron, 1 lemon, 3 eggs, beaten, 1/2 cup Vin Santo wine, 1/2 cup Anisette liqueur.

Mix the spelt wheat, milk, sugar, almonds, candied citron. Also add the whole lemon that has been poked with a fork so that the juice will be released during cooking. Cook according to wheat package instructions. Cool completely and remove the lemon. Mix in the beaten eggs. Pour into a buttered 2-quart baking dish and bake at 180°C/350°F for at least 30 minutes or until golden. As soon as removed from oven, pour the liqueur over the top. Serve warm. This dessert should be eaten within 1-2 days or the smelt wheat will become hard.

DOLCE FIRENZE
FLORENTINE BREAD PUDDING

◆

4 slices Italian bread (Tuscan unsalted), 1/4 cup butter, 1/4 cup raisins, plumped in hot water then squeezed to remove excess water, 3/4 cup sugar, 3 eggs, 2 cups of milk mixed with some whipping cream, grated rind of 1 lemon, 1 cup Marsala or Vin Santo wine.

Toast the bread slices. (They should be just right: not too thin or too thick). Liberally butter a 1-quart rectangular high-sided baking dish. Put the toasted bread in the bottom and pour the Marsala wine on top. Briefly beat the eggs, sugar, milk and cream together. Pour the egg mixture over the toast and sprinkle with the plumped raisins and grated lemon rind. Bake in a 190°C/375°F pre-heated oven for 45 minutes. Serve warm. Traces of this simple but hearty dessert can be found still in medieval Florentine cookbooks. It was a popular and approved dessert during the Medici reign although it was simple, and even 'rustic'. I see Florentine witticism in its name. Is 'dolce' (sweet) used as a substantive noun or as an adjective referring to Florence?

DOLCE RICOTTA
RICOTTA DESSERT

◆

16 oz. (2 cups) fresh ricotta cheese, 1/2 cup sugar, 2 teaspoons powdered coffee - fresh coffee that is ground so finely that it resembles cocoa powder - ladyfinger cookies (you can also use 'Zuccherini' - see recipe).

Put the ricotta in a bowl and mix well until completely smooth. Add the sugar, mix until smooth. Add the powdered coffee, mix to smooth. Cover the bowl and set it in the refrigerator for at least two hours. This should be eaten cold accompanied by ladyfingers or zuccherini.

DOLCE RUSTICO DI BIETOLE
RUSTIC SWISS CHARD DESSERT
◆

1 1/2 cups flour, 2/3 cup softened butter, 3/4 cup sugar, 2 eggs, separated, pinch of salt, 1 lb. fresh Swiss chard, 1/4 cup pine nuts, 1/4 cup raisins, plumped in hot water then squeezed to remove excess water, 1 teaspoon each: cinnamon and nutmeg.

On a flat work surface, blend the flour, very soft butter, 1/4 cup of the sugar, egg yolks and salt. Knead with your hands until smooth and elastic. Form a ball and set aside, covered by a cloth for an hour. Clean the chard, removing the hard center and cook it in a pot, covered, without adding water; it will cook in the drops left on the leaves from washing. When

cooked, squeeze it to remove excess liquid and chop. Sautee the chard in a pan with some butter briefly. Put the chards in a bowl along with the 1/2 cup remaining sugar, pine nuts and plumped raisins. Mix with a wooden spoon. Add the spices. Cut the dough into two pieces – one with two-thirds of the dough and the other with one-third – roll out the larger piece to a height of 1/4-inch.
Butter and flour a 9" springform pan and fill with the rolled out dough: let the edges hang over. Pour in the chard mixture. Roll out the smaller ball of dough and cover the pie. Crimp or flute the edges to seal. Brush the top with the leftover egg whites that have been slightly beaten. Bake in a pre-heated 220°C/425°F oven for about 20 minutes. Cool and serve when still warm.

DOLCETTI DI CANNELLA
CINNAMON BARS

36

2 1/4 cups flour, 4 eggs, 1 cup sugar, 1 1/2 teaspoons cinnamon, 1/4 cup raisins, plumped in hot water then squeezed to remove excess water, 1/8 cup pistachio nuts, 1 cup milk, warmed, 2 teaspoons baking powder, powdered sugar for dusting, butter.

Put the pistachios in a saucepan with some water and cook just to boiling. Drain, peel and chop into large pieces. Set aside. Beat the eggs with the sugar until thick and smooth. Slowly add the flour, while still beating, then the cinnamon. When well blended, add the pistachios and prepared raisins. Dissolve the baking powder in the warmed milk and beat it into the batter. Pour the batter into a buttered 9" x 13" rectangular pan and bake it in a 160°C/325°F pre-heated oven for 40 minutes. Turn the cake out onto a cooling rack. When cold, slice lengthwise into palm-wide strips that you'll then slice into 1/2-inch bars. Sprinkle with powdered sugar and enjoy them with a good cup of coffee.

DOLCETTI DI SEMOLINO DI S. GIUSEPPE
SEMOLINA TREATS

◆

RECIPE FOR 12-15 1/2-CUP CUSTARD CUPS — OR MUFFIN TIN: 1 qt. milk, grated peel of 1/2 lemon, 1 cup semolina flour, 1/2 cup chopped walnuts, pinch of salt, 3/4 cup sugar, 1/4 cup softened butter, 2 eggs + 2 yolks.

In a saucepan: boil the milk and

grated lemon peel. Slowly add while whisking the semolina so that it doesn't become lumpy. Cook over a low flame for about 10 minutes, whisking constantly. Remove from heat and add 1/4 cup of the chopped walnuts, salt and sugar. Cook another 5 minutes.
Cool. Add the whole eggs, yolks and butter. Pour the batter into buttered custard cups and sprinkle the remaining walnuts on top. Cook in a hot water bath for 20 minutes in a 190°C/375°F pre-heated oven. Turn out the puddings only when cold. Enjoy them accompanied by rice fritters ('frittelle di riso') and a glass of Vin Santo.

DONZELLINE DOLCI
SWEET FRIED DOUGH

1 cup flour, 2 tablespoons sugar, 2 tablespoons softened butter, 2 eggs, pinch of salt, 1 teaspoon fennel seeds, 1 cup brandy, olive oil for frying.

Put the flour onto a flat work surface and mix in the butter, eggs, sugar, salt, fennel seeds and, lastly, the brandy with your hands. Knead the dough until it is elastic and pretty hard. If necessary, flour your hands often. Set aside, covered, for 30 minutes. Roll out the dough to a height of 1/2-inch. Cut the dough into 1 1/2-inch strips using a zigzag-edged roll cutter (looks like a pizza cutter but has a serrated edged blade). Form

the strips into little donuts. Fry the strips in boiling oil – remember, to fry well, the oil must be abundant and the 'donzelline' need to float in it while frying. Remove from oil when golden, drain and place on absorbent paper.

Sprinkle with sugar and serve hot (or cold). Children adore these... but I know some adults who wou<ld gladly become kids again for a plate!
This simple snack is nutritious and stores well in a hermetic jar.

DURELLI
HARD ALMOND COOKIES

◆

2 3/4 cups flour, 2 cups sugar, 1/2 cup honey (mille fiori), 1/2 cup sweet chopped almonds, 1/4 cup bitter chopped almonds, 2 teaspoons baking soda, pinch of fresh ground black pepper.

Mix the flour, sugar and pepper together in a large bowl. Add the honey, mix, and then the two types of almonds. Lastly, add the baking soda.

Mix until stiff and sticky. If necessary, add a little water. Set aside for 30 minutes to rest. Form small 1-inch long cylinders and place them on a buttered and floured baking sheet. Bake in a preheated 190°C/375°F oven for 20 minutes. Serve these while still warm with some Passito wine or Rosolio liqueur.

FARINATA DI GRANTURCO
CON LE NOCI
POLENTA WITH WALNUTS

◆

1 qt. water, 3 tablespoon sugar, 1/2 teaspoon salt, 2 cups corn flour (polenta), 1/2 cup chopped walnuts, 1 branch fresh rosemary, olive oil.

Mix the water with the salt and sugar in a large pot and bring it to a boil. Remove the pot from the heat and while stirring constantly with a wooden spoon pour in the polenta. Return the pot to the heat and cook over a medium flame, stirring constantly for 45 minutes. While the polenta is cooking, heat a little olive oil with the rosemary and the chopped walnuts and cook for a few minutes. Add to the polenta. Cook another 10 minutes, stirring vigorously. Pour the polenta onto a marble counter or a greased shallow-sided tray. This dish is excellent just made accompanied by some good red wine... I think that this dessert is best when served cold: sliced thickly, fried golden in olive oil and sprinkled with sugar.

An afternoon snack from long ago that could once again find a spot on our tables... as a sweet ending to a child's birthday party.

FIAMME FREDDE
FROZEN PUDDING FLAMBÉ

◆

1 Jelly Roll Cake (Pan di Spagna, see recipe B), 2 cups Limoncello liqueur or Latte di Vecchia.

FOR THE CREAM: 2 cups whipping cream, 3/4 cup powdered sugar with vanilla, 2 egg yolks, slightly beaten, 1/8 cup chopped candied citron, 1/4 cup chopped candied orange, 1 1/2 cups toasted mixed hazelnuts and almonds, 1/8 cup un-sweetened cocoa powder, 5 oz. dark chocolate, 1/8 cup butter, 2 tablespoons cooking alcohol (90% proof).

Prepare the cake and set it aside to cool completely.

Line the mold: Slice the cake into thin strips and line a 2-quart pudding mold (also called a 'zuccotto' mold here). Brush the cake with the liqueur mixed with a little water. Set aside. Prepare the cream: whip the cream and vanilla sugar to stiff peaks and divide it into two bowls. In the first bowl beat in the egg yolks, add the candied fruits and all but 1/4 cup of the toasted nuts. Pour this into the cake-lined mold and place it in the fridge. In the second bowl of whipped cream: stir in the cocoa powder and shave in about an ounce of the dark chocolate. Stir gently. Put this on top of the first layer of cream and level it off with a rubber spatula. Sprinkle with the remaining nuts and cover the pudding with aluminum foil and place it in the freezer for at least 3 hours. At least 2 hours prior to serving: melt the remaining chocolate with the butter and a few drops of the liqueur in a saucepan over simmering water.

Un-mold the pudding onto a platter and pour on the melted chocolate slowly and evenly so that it looks like a seal over the entire top.

Place it in the freezer for one hour. Remove the pudding from the freezer 30 minutes before serving and wet the cake with more of the liqueur.

In a saucepan, heat up some of the liqueur with the 2 tablespoons of cooking alcohol. Light the heated liqueur with a match and carefully spoon the burning liquid over the top of the pudding... for a lovely 'flaming' dessert.

FICATTOLE
FRIED DOUGH

◆

12 oz. bread dough (Pasta di pane, see recipe C), olive oil, sugar (or salt).

Set the prepared bread dough aside to rise until it is large and fluffy.

Break the dough into small balls and roll them into small cylinders. Fry them in olive oil until golden and drip-dry on absorbent paper.

Sprinkle each 'ficattola' with either sugar or salt - either ways is good, depending on your taste. During winter, farmers served salted 'ficattole' with their dinners to make them more abundant, to the children they were served with sugar when celebrating the wine harvest... they're wonderful both ways.

FICATTOLE RICCHE
DEL VALDARNO
FIG AND NUT TART

◆

1 1/2 cups flour, 1 cup softened butter, 1 cup sugar, 4 egg yolks, 1 cup dried beans, 8 oz. dried figs, chopped, 1/4 cup chopped candied orange peel, 2/3 cup mixed toasted almonds and hazelnuts, 2 tablespoons honey, 2 tablespoons bitter orange marmalade.

Mound the flour onto a flat surface and form a crater in the center. Add the butter – sliced into small pieces – the egg yolks and sugar. Knead briefly until a ball is formed.

Cover with aluminum foil and set in the fridge for 30 minutes. Butter and flour a 10" tart tin. Roll out the prepared dough to 1/2-inch thick and line the tin; fold and crimp the edges.

Bake, lined with oven paper and the dried beans, in a 220°C/425°F pre-heated oven for 20 minutes. While the tart is baking, put the chopped almonds, hazelnuts, dried figs and candied orange peel in a mixing bowl and blend them together with the honey and bitter orange marmalade. Fill the prepared tart – remove the beans and the paper – with the prepared fruits and level them out using a spatula. Return the tart to the oven for an additional 30 minutes. Serve cooled. This is a real delicacy when accompanied by some Rosolio liqueur.

FICATTOLE SBIAGGINATE DEL CHIANTI
FRESH FIG FOCACCIA

◆

1 lb. bread dough, 1/2 cup honey (mille fiori), 1 lb. ripe figs, oil.

Knead the prepared bread dough with half of the honey until smooth and elastic. Roll it out flat to the size of a 15" jellyroll pan.
It should be about an inch in height. Place it on an oiled sheet and, with floured hands, make sure that the dough is fitted nicely to the entire tray.
Wash the figs, peel them and slice them in half. 'Squash' them onto the surface of the focaccia and pour the remaining honey on top.
Let rest for 30 minutes before baking in a 220°C/425°F pre-heated oven for one hour. In the Chianti aerea the name of this fociaccia contains the word 'sbiagginare' which means 'schiacciare' – or rather 'to squash'.

FICHI AL VIN SANTO
FIGS WITH VIN SANTO WINE

16 fresh, ripe green figs, 3/4 cup Vin Santo wine, 3/4 cup white wine, 1 teaspoon sugar, fresh mint leaves.

41

Delicately peel the figs and put them on a serving tray with high borders. Sprinkle the sugar on top and wet them with the Vin Santo wine.

Refrigerate for 1 hour. Wash the mint and mix it with the white wine. Pour this on top of the figs. Let marinade in the refrigerator for at least another hour.

At country parties we enjoyed these figs served with a large tray of cured meats: Sbriciolona (fennel flavored salame), salame cut in thick slices and Buristo (cured sausage prepared with pig's blood and spices).

FICHI CANDITI
DELLA CONTADINA
FARMWOMAN'S CANDIED FIGS

◆

2.2 lbs. figs (should still have a white drop of serum at the stem), 1 1/2 cups sugar, 2 lemons, 1 cup Vin Santo wine.

Delicately peel the figs and place them in a baking pan. Grate the rind of one of the lemons and squeeze the other. Sprinkle the figs with the sugar and grated peel and pour the lemon juice on top and lastly, pour on the Vin Santo. Bake in a 160°C/325°F pre-heated oven for 20 minutes until golden brown in color. Serve cold and/or store them in a jar with a hermetic seal.

FICHI GOLOSI DEI BENEDETTINI
SWEET FIGS – BENEDICTINE STYLE

📷

1 vanilla bean, 1 cup milk, 2 eggs, separated, 1/4 cup sugar, 2.2 lbs. ripe figs, 1/4 cup flour, 1/8 cup unsalted pistachio nuts, 1 cup whipping cream, 1 tablespoon sweet cocoa powder.

Boil the milk with the sugar bean for a few minutes then set aside to cool. Remove the vanilla bean. In a large mixing bowl beat the egg yolks with the sugar until just thickened.

Add the flour, then little by little the milk. Pour into a large saucepan and cook, stirring slowly but continuously, until thick. Cool. Cut the tops of the figs and empty as much of the pulp as you can without breaking the skin.

Put them in the fridge to cool. Mix the fig pulp into the cream mixture, fill the prepared skins and place them in the refrigerator.

Prepare the pistachios: boil briefly in water, drain and remove the skins. Chop them a little and mix them with the whipping cream. To serve: dust the figs with the cocoa powder and pour the whipping cream on top.

FILONE CON I CANDITI
CANDIED FRUIT STRUDEL

◆

1/2 recipe flaky pastry dough (Pasta Sfoglia, see recipe F), 1 cup whipping cream, 1/4 cup sugar, 1/4 cup apple jelly, 1/4 cup mixed chopped candied fruit, 1 egg white, 1/8 cup finely chopped almonds (powder-like).

Prepare the flaky pastry dough. Whip the cream with half of the sugar and put it in the refrigerator. Roll out the dough very thinly and spread apple jelly on top, then sprinkle with the chopped candied fruit. Roll into a cylinder.

Briefly whip the egg white with the remaining sugar and fold in the chopped almonds.

Place the cylinder on a buttered and floured baking sheet and brush the top

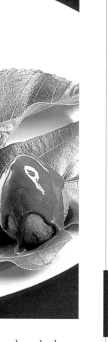

with the egg white mixture. Bake in 220°C/425°F pre-heated oven for 30 minutes until golden. Serve cold with the whipped cream.

FIORI DI ZUCCHINE DOLCI DELLA VIA VIUCCIA
FRIED ZUCCHINI FLOWERS WITH PEACH FILLING

◆

20 zucchini flowers, 2 peaches, ripe and sweet, ca. 10 ladyfingers, crumbled finely, 1 egg, 1/4 cup sugar, oil for frying.
BATTER: 3/4 cup flour, 3 egg whites, 1 1/2 qts. milk, pinch of salt, 1/4 cup powdered sugar.

Choose large, fresh zucchini flowers. Carefully wash them and dry them with paper towels.
Peel the peaches and cut them into little pieces that you'll put in a bowl along with the egg and sugar and crumbled ladyfingers. Mix well with a whisk. Carefully fill the zucchini flowers with the peach mixture.
You may widen the opening with your fingers to aide you.
Prepare the batter: mix the flour and milk together in a large bowl. Add a pinch of salt. Beat the egg whites to stiff peaks and fold them into the milk mixture until just smooth.
Dip each flower in the batter and fry them in abundant boiling oil.
Cook both sides until golden in color, drain and dry on absorbent paper. Put the fried flowers on a serving platter and sprinkle with powdered sugar.
Serve while still hot, for a delicious and unusual treat; this is a different way to serve zucchini flowers.

FOCACCIA D'AUTUNNO
AUTUMN FOCACCIA

◆

1 1/3 cups spelt wheat, 2 teaspoons baking powder, 1/4 cup sugar, 3/4 cup softened butter, 3 eggs, 1/2 cup milk, 1/2 cup grapes, 1 teaspoon cinnamon, 1/8 teaspoon nutmeg, 5 tablespoons apricot jam + 1 tablespoon water (heat, pass though a sieve to remove all pieces).

Boil the spelt wheat according to the directions found on the package, drain well. Puree the wheat, then place it in a bowl with the sugar, baking powder and a pinch of salt.
Blend in the softened butter gently, stirring with a wooden spoon.
Whip the eggs and pour them along with the milk into the mixture; blend with a whisk and add the spices. Pour into an 8" buttered baking pan.
De-stem and squash the grapes and press them onto the surface of the batter. Bake in a pre-heated 170°C/325°F oven.
If you'd like: as soon as the focaccia comes out of the oven, brush the top with the apricot jam (dissolved in a little water over a low flame).
In winter I like to use orange jelly which I've flavored with a laurel leaf.

FRAGOLE AL VINO ROSSO
STRAWBERRIES IN RED WINE

◆

1 lb. Strawberries, 3/4 cup sugar, 2 cups red wine, fresh mint leaves.

Wash the strawberries and put them in a bowl with the sugar, red wine (a young and fresh red wine, such as 'novello') and mix gently. Add the mint leaves and set in

the refrigerator to marinade for at least fifteen minutes before serving the strawberries to your guests.

FRITTELLE
ALLO ZIBIBBO E PINOLI
FRIED RAISIN
AND PINE NUT DOUGH

◆

1 oz. fresh compressed active beer yeast, 1/2 cup flour, 1/2 cup + 2 1/2 cups milk, 1/2 cup Arborio rice, 1 tablespoon sugar, 3 eggs, 1/4 cup sultana raisins plumped in hot water then squeezed to remove excess, 1/8 cup pine nuts, finely grated rind 1 lemon, pinch of salt, olive oil for frying, powdered sugar.

Dissolve 1/4 cup of the flour and yeast in a bowl with the 1/2 cup of warm milk and knead to form a smooth dough. Set aside to rise for 45 minutes. Boil the remaining 2-1/2 cups of milk with the rice and sugar. Cook over medium heat for about 20 minutes.
Pour the rice into a large bowl and let cool. Add the remaining flour, the egg and yolks and mix until blended. Add the prepared yeast and incorporate it gently. Add the raisins, pine nuts, grated lemon peel and salt.
Mix well and set aside for 30 minutes. Fill a large pot halfway up with frying oil and heat to boiling. Drop the dough in by spoonfuls.

44

Cook, turning until golden. Remove, drip and dry on absorbent paper. Sprinkle with powdered sugar. They're good cold but unforgettable when still warm.

FRITTELLE DA MERENDA
RAISIN AND ORANGE FRITTERS

◆

2 1/2 cups flour, pinch of salt, grated rind 1 orange, 5 eggs, separated, 1/2 cup raisins, plumped in hot water then squeezed to remove excess water, 1/2 cup sugar, oil for frying.

Put the flour and salt in a bowl. Add enough water to make a smooth batter. In a frying pan, add a little oil and heat. Pour the batter in and cook it, turning once, being careful that it doesn't become crunchy; do not overcook.
Put the 'frittata' in a bowl and break it up with your hands, then with a knife so that it is completely shredded.
Add the grated orange peel and slightly beaten egg yolks and mix until smooth. Add the raisins.
Beat the egg whites until they form stiff peaks and fold them into the frittata mixture. Pour some oil into a pan and heat. Drop the batter into the hot oil by spoonfuls. Cook to golden on both sides. Dry the fritters on absorbent paper and sprinkle with the sugar. As a child these fritters were made with left-over 'tondone' – what I called frittate.
This was made primarily to add to the dinner fare. It was usually flavored with some fresh chopped sage or laurel leaves. Since our lesson is, "don't throw anything away", this recipe makes a truly delicious afternoon snack using leftovers. It's usually accompanied by some home-made jam.

FRITTELLE DI CASTAGNE
CHESTNUT FRITTERS

◆

1 1/2 cups chestnut flour, 1/4 cup raisins, plumped in hot water then squeezed to remove excess water, 1/8 cup pine nuts, a few leaves of fresh rosemary, pinch of salt, 1/2 cup sugar, olive oil for frying.

In a bowl mix the flour and plumped raisins, pine nuts and rosemary. Add a pinch of salt and enough water to make a smooth, dense paste.
Fill a pan with frying oil and bring it to a boil. Drop the paste into the boiling oil by spoonfuls. Cook each side several minutes until golden. Drain well and dry on absorbent paper. Sprinkle with sugar and eat immediately.
Note: These fritters are perfect only when served just made and still hot. When they become cold the chestnut flour will begin releasing the oil, thus making them heavy and greasy.

FRITTELLE
DI FARINA DOLCE
FRIED CHESTNUT CAKES

◆

1/4 cup raisins, 1 1/2 cup chestnut flour, 1 cup water, 1 tablespoon oil, pinch of salt, olive oil for frying.

Plump the raisins in hot water before starting. In the meantime, put the chestnut flour in a bowl and slowly pour in the water, mixing slowly with a whisk so as to prevent lumps. Slowly add the drained and squeezed raisins, salt and oil until well mixed. Fill a pan with frying oil and heat it to boiling. Put the mixture into the oil by spoonful, making sure that both sides are evenly browned.

45

When removing the cakes from the oil, make sure they drip adequately and that they're well dried on absorbent paper. These are good served either hot or cold and are a good snack even the next day.

FRITTELLE DI MELE
APPLE FRITTERS

1 1/2 lbs. baking apples (renette type), 1/2 cup flour, water, 1 egg, oil for frying, 1/2 cup sugar.

Core the apples and slice them into thick rings. Prepare the batter: mix the flour with enough water to form a thickened paste and mix in the egg.
Heat some oil (enough to cover the bottom of a frying pan). Dip the apple slices in the batter and fry them just until golden on both sides.
Dry them on absorbent paper. When cold, sprinkle with sugar. Variation: an unusual but delicious variation is to substitute the water with some vino novello, but obviously, this is only available in autumn. The flavor will be nicely tart and have a delicate aroma.

FRITTELLE DI RISO
MARDI GRAS FRIED RICE BALLS
◆

1 lb. Arborio rice, 1 qt. milk, 1/2 qt. water, 1 orange cut into slices, 1/2 lemon cut into slices, 1 1/2 cups sugar, 3 eggs + 2 yolks, 2 tablespoons flour, 1/2 cup Vin Santo wine, 3 teaspoons baking powder, olive oil.

Mix the cold water, milk and rice together in a large pot and add the orange and lemon slices.
Cook over a moderate flame, stirring of-

ten, for about 45 minutes until almost all of the liquid is absorbed. Cool and remove the orange and lemon slices. Beat the eggs and yolks together. Little by little add the Vin Santo wine, flour and baking powder, to the rice. Set aside at least 8 hours. Fry, turning gently with a spoon and fork, tablespoon-size balls in very hot olive oil until golden. Drain and dry on absorbent paper. Sprinkle with sugar and enjoy them hot.

FRITTELLE DI S. GIUSEPPE
ALLA MODA DI GROSSETO
ST. JOSEPH'S
FRIED BREAD DOUGH
◆

2 cups water, 3 tablespoons sugar, pinch of salt, 2 tablespoons oil, grated peel 1 lemon, 1 cup flour, 2 eggs, 1/2 teaspoon baking soda, olive oil for frying, sugar.

Mix the water, sugar, salt, lemon peel and oil in a saucepan. Bring to a boil and add the flour. Make sure you mix well with a whisk so that the mixture doesn't get lumpy. Stir until completely smooth and set aside for 20 minutes. Slowly add the beaten eggs and when well blended add baking soda. Stir well and set aside to rest 10 minutes.
Heat a pan of olive oil and fry the dough by dropping in teaspoon-size clumps. Turn until all sides are golden.
Dripdrain and set on absorbent paper. Sprinkle with sugar. These are good only when served hot.

FRITTELLINE DI BORRAGINE
FRIED BORAGE LEAVES
◆

3/4 lb. washed and dried borage leaves, 1 egg, 2/3 cup flour, 1/4 cup sugar, 1 cup milk, olive oil for frying.

Clean, wash and dry in a towel the borage leaves. Set aside. Prepare the batter: mix the milk, flour and lastly the egg. Mix with a spoon until completely smooth. Fill a pan with frying oil and bring to a boil. Dip tufts of leaves into the batter and fry. When nicely golden and crunchy, remove from oil, drip-dry on absorbent paper and sprinkle with sugar. These are de-licious just cooked and lose their fragrance if eaten cold. The Borage (a humble plant) grows in the wild and can be used for many things: its blue flowers are used to aromatize and color white wine vinegar..

FRUTTINI DI FIRENZE
CANDIED QUINCE

◆

2.2 lbs. quince apples, 2.2 lbs. sugar, 2 lemons, butter.

Peel and core the apples and put them in a large bowl with the juice of 1 1/2 lemons. Now, put them into a large pot with the juice of 1/2 lemon, 1/2 cup of water and the sliced peel of 1 lemon (remember to use only the yellow part of the peel).

Cook over a moderate flame stirring often until the apples are cooked. Puree – without the lemon peel. Put the puree back in the saucepan and add the sugar.

Continue cooking on a low flame, stirring often to ensure that the puree doesn't burn or stick to the pan, for 1 hour. When the quince puree has become thick and brown in color, pour it onto a buttered 15" jellyroll pan. Even it out with a steel spatula dipped in water. Let cool and harden. Slice into small rectangles and wrap each one in oiled waxed paper, making sure to seal the edges carefully. These store well in hermetically sealed jars.

Gattò Aretino
Filled Cake Roll – Arezzo Style

📷

For the cake: 1 1/2 cups sugar, 6 eggs, seperated, 2/3 cup flour, 1/4 cup potato flour, 2 teaspoons baking powder, 1/2 cup Alkermes liqueur, diluted with some water.

For the cream filling: 2 egg yolks, 1/3 cup sugar, 2 cups milk, 2 teaspoons flour.

For the chocolate sauce: 1/4 cup butter, 2-1/2 oz. dark chocolate, 1/2 cup milk.

Prepare the cake: sift the potato flour, white flour and baking powder together and set aside.

Beat the yolks with the sugar until smooth and thick. Set aside. Beat the whites to stiff peaks. Fold them into the yolks, then fold in the sifted flours. Blend to form a smooth dough. Pour into a 15" jellyroll rectangular cake pan that has been lined with oven paper and bake at 190°C/375°F for 30 minutes. Cool completely.

Prepare the cream: put the yolk and sugar directly into a saucepan and whisk until smooth. Whisk in the flour and milk. Cook at low heat while stirring continuously until very thick.

Set aside to cool. Prepare the chocolate sauce: place the chocolate, butter and milk into a small saucepan over a pan full of simmering water until completely melted.

Set aside to cool. Wet the surface of the cooled cake with Alkermes liqueur. Spread a layer of cream then a layer of chocolate sauce evenly on the cake. Gently roll the cake, using the paper liner to aide you, into a log. Seal the ends with the paper and set the cake in the refrigerator until 30 minutes before serving. This cake is often garnished with whipping cream that has been sweetened with honey (mille fiori).

Ghirighio
Chestnut Flat Bread

◆

2 tablespoons olive oil, 1 branch of fresh rosemary, 11/3 cups chestnut flour, 1 cup fresh ricotta cheese, 1/4 cup pine nuts, 1/4 cup chopped walnuts, 1/4 cup raisins.

Heat the olive oil and the rosemary branch in a small pan.

As soon as it smokes, remove from heat and cool – discard the rosemary. (Before starting, make sure that your chestnut

flour is very fresh and not from last year; it can be found after mid-November). Place the flour in a bowl and while stirring with a wooden spoon, then slowly add the other ingredients, except for the ricotta.

Alternate the dry ingredients with the rosemary-flavored oil. Grease the bottom of an 8" rectangular baking tin and pour in the mixture.

Bake in a hot pre-heated 200°C/400°F oven for 30 minutes.

This is delicious either warm or cold. What distinguishes this from its close cousin Castagnaccio, is that it is served with fresh ricotta – the fresh, fresh kind that melts in your mouth!

GIALLETTI
CORNMEAL COOKIES

◆

1 1/2 cups fine yellow polenta flour, 3/4 cup white flour, 1/3 cup butter, softened, 3/4 cup sugar, 2 eggs + 1 yolk, slightly beaten, 1 scant cup milk.

Sift the white and yellow flours together on to a work surface, forming a crater in the center where you'll put the softened butter, cut into pieces, the sugar and beaten eggs. Add the egg yolk last. Continue kneading and slowly add the milk, little by little. Once all of the ingredients are blended knead vigorously until the dough becomes smooth and solid. Form a ball, cover it with foil and set in the fridge for 30 minutes. Roll out the dough on a floured surface to 1/2-inch thick. Cut out rounds (with a cutter or a glass with a small opening) and place them on a lightly buttered baking sheet. Bake in a 190°C/375°F pre-heated oven for thirty minutes. Cool.

These are delicious served with home-made liqueurs and store well closed in jars with hermetic seals.

that deposits on the bottom of the pot when making ricotta cheese – so it may be substituted with 'raveggiolo', a sweet-er fresh cheese. Put the cheese in a bowl and pour the Alkermes and sugar on top. Blend with a whisk. Sprinkle the grated peel on top and refrigerate.

Serve cold at the end of the meal or as an afternoon snack accompanied by home-made cookies.

GIUNCATA ALLA TOSCANA
SWEETENED RAVEGGIOLO CHEESE
◆

8 oz. fresh 'giuncata' or 'raveggiolo' cheese, 1/2 cup Alkermes liqueur, 2 tablespoons sugar, 1 lemon.

It is difficult to find 'giuncata' cheese – that is the milk part, following curdling,

LATTAIOLO
COOKED MILK DESSERT

4 eggs, 1/4 cup flour, 1 qt. whole milk, pinch of each: ground anise seed, cinnamon and salt, grated peel of 1 lemon, 1 tablespoon powdered sugar, butter.

Beat the eggs in a bowl and slowly add

the flour, milk, spices, lemon peel and salt. Beat well after each addition.

Grease an oval 9 1/2" x 5" baking dish, pour in the batter and bake in a pre-heated 190°C/375°F oven for 30 minutes. Cool and turn out onto a serving tray. Dust with the powdered sugar.

This tasty dessert is even better served with a sugar caramel that is drizzled over each portion.

MANDORLATO
ALMOND BRITTLE

1/2 lb. almonds, 1 cup sugar, grated rind of 1 lemon, oil, 2 tablespoons water.

Briefly boil the almonds in water to loosen the skin. Drain, rub with a towel to remove the skins. Chop nuts into large pieces and place them on a baking sheet. Dry them in the oven – on the lowest setting – for about 10 minutes. In a large saucepan (copper is best) melt the sugar with two tablespoons of water, the almonds and grated rind.

Cook stirring continuously over a very low flame. Be careful that the brittle doesn't become bitter due to over cooking – it should be a nice brown (candy thermometer reading 135°C/275°F).

Oil a low-sided baking pan and pour the brittle into it. Spread evenly using a wet knife. When completely cooled and hardened, break the brittle into pieces and serve.

If the brittle sticks to the pan, place the bottom in some hot water and it will come right out.

MARMELLATA DI CASTAGNE ALL'USO DI PISTOIA
CHESTNUT JAM – PISTOIA STYLE
◆

FOR 3 TO 4 1/2-CUP JARS: 3 lbs. fresh chestnuts, peel of 1 orange, peel of 1 lemon, 3-4 laurel leaves, 1 branch fresh fennel, 4 cups sugar, pinch of salt.

Fill a large pot with cold water: add the chestnuts, orange and lemon peels, laurel and fennel leaves. Cook for about an hour. Drain, remove all of the peel and leaves, peel and puree the chestnuts. Put the chestnut puree in a pot and add the sugar, salt and about 1 cup of water. Cook over a very low flame, stirring constantly, for about 45 minutes. Pour into prepared canning jars. If you're a real gourmand, pour a little rum on top before sealing. You can keep them as is and use them within a month or seal them in a water bath for longer storage.

52

MARMELLATA DI FICHI DOTTATI
GREEN FIG JAM
◆

RECIPE FOR 6 1/2-CUP JARS: 4 1/2 lbs. ripe green figs, 3 lbs. sugar, 2 lemons.

Clean and peel the figs, leaving some of the peel, and cut them in half. Put them in a large pot. Cook over a low flame for about 30 minutes, stirring with a wooden spoon. Add the sugar and lemon peels and continue stirring. Cook for about two hours, stirring often. If you want you can puree them but you must do so while the jam is still hot. If not water sealing, use within a month. This jam is delicious, however, left in whole pieces because it exalts the flavor of the figs. My

family and I make this together every year but, it always signifies the end of summer...

MARMELLATA DI MELE
APPLE BUTTER
◆

RECIPE FOR 6 1/2-CUP JARS: 3 lbs. golden delicious apples, 1 cup sugar, grated peel 1 lemon + some of the juice.

Peel, core and slice the apples into thin slices. Put them in a saucepan and mix in the sugar and some fresh squeezed lemon juice. Cook over low heat for about 30 minutes, mixing and breaking up the fruit often. Add the grated rind and keep cooking the apples, stirring often, another hour. Depending on the type of apple (harder or softer) continue cooking for another 30 minutes. How can you know that the jam is ready? Test by dropping a teaspoonful into a glass of cold water, if the jam drops and remains solid then it's ready. Pour into prepared jars. Use within one-month or water seal.

MATTONELLA RICCA ALLA FRUTTA DELLE SUORE DI S. MARTA
THE NUNS OF ST. MARTA MIXED FRUIT PUDDING

1 lb. Golden delicious apples, 1/2 lb. ripe Bartlett pears, 1/2 lb. ripe strawberries, washed and de-stemmed, 1 banana, 3/4 cup sugar, 2 cups white wine, 1/2 cup dried pitted prunes plumped in hot water, 1/4 cup chopped citron, 1/4 cup rum, pinch of cinnamon, ladyfinger cookies (about 16 oz.), 3 tablespoons Vin Santo wine.

Wash, peel and core the apples and pears. Chop them up and place them in a large saucepan with the strawberries, banana and sugar. As soon as the fruit begins to boil, add the white wine. Stir with a wooden spoon. Add the dried prunes, chopped citron, rum and cinnamon. Cook, over a low flame, for 15 minutes, stirring often until the fruit resembles jam. Make sure that the fruit doesn't dry by adding a little water if necessary.
Set aside to cool. Place the ladyfingers in the bottom of a serving bowl and wet them with the Vin Santo. If this is for a children's party, you may dilute the wine with some water. Spread all of the fruit on the cookies and top them with more la-dyfingers. Press down gently with your hands, cover and place the bowl in the re-frigerator – in the coldest section – for at least 2 hours before serving. This dessert can also be turned out onto a platter – loosen it by placing a hot wet towel on the serving bowl when turning. Decorate with fresh fruit and dollops of whipped cream.

MELE IN FORNO
BAKED APPLES
◆

4 golden delicious apples, 2 tablespoons sugar, 1/4 cup soft butter, melted, 1/2 cup water.
VARIATION: 1/2 scant cup raisins, 2 tablespoons honey (acacia)

Using an apple corer, remove the center of the apples, then make a cut in the peel around the fattest part. Place the apples in an ovenproof pan, and fill the centers with the sugar. Mix the melted butter with the water and pour them over the tops. Bake at 170°C/325°F for about 45 minutes, wetting them often with the juices. They should be soft but still retain their shape when cooked.

Variation: fill the centers with honey, instead of sugar, and raisins, which have been plumped-up in hot water for 10 minutes.

MELE IN FORNO RIVESTITE
APPLE DUMPLINGS

4 golden delicious apples, 3 tablespoons raisins, 4 tablespoons honey (acacia), 1/4 cup butter, 1 recipe pastry dough (pasta frolla, see recipe C).

This is a delicious variation on simple baked apples. This dessert was traditionally made in an old pastry shop (known as a 'laboratorio di pasticceria') located in the heart of Florence in an area known as San Giovanni.

The apples were prepared according to the recipe for baked apples (see recipe "Mele in Forno") then wrapped in a thin layer of pastry dough and closed at the top like a sack... brushed with egg yolk, then baked another twenty minutes at 190°C/375°F, transforming them into a tastier, richer and highly popular sweet that was prepared to celebrate the local festivals. Who, like me, had the fortune to taste those incredible 'dressed' apples will never forget the unforgettable smell that wafted throughout the quarter on such occasions!

MIELATELLI DI ASCIANO
ASCIANO HONEY BALLS

◆

2 1/2 cups flour, 1/2 cup melted butter, 6 eggs, slightly beaten, 1 cup honey (acacia), grated peel of 1 lemon, oil for frying.

On a flat surface mound the flour to form a crater. Add the melted butter, beaten eggs, half of the honey and knead energetically. Add the grated lemon peel. When well kneaded cover with a cloth and set aside for 30 minutes. Roll out the dough – leave thick - onto a floured surface. Cut out cylinders and roll them in the palm of your hand to form small balls that you'll then roll in flour. Heat oil to boiling in a pan and fry the cookies, a few at a time, until golden. Drain and dry on absorbent paper. Melt the remaining honey over a very low flame and dip each cookie (using a long wooden stick) then place them on a serving platter. Form the cookies into a pyramid. Pour any remaining honey on top and let cool before serving. These are often garnished with candied fruit or colored sugar at parties.

MIGLIACCIO O CASTAGNACCIO
CHESTNUT PANCAKE

3/4 cup chestnut flour (known as 'farina dolce'), 1 cup water, 8 tablespoons olive oil, 1 handful each: pine nuts and raisins (plumped in hot water), olive oil, rosemary.

Put the 'farina dolce' (called sweet be-

cause good chestnut flour, found only towards the end of November, is so sweet and pasty that it's unnecessary to add sugar) in a bowl with two tablespoons of oil and whisk. Slowly add cold water until the batter is fluid and smooth. Set aside 30 minutes. Prepare some rosemary oil by heating the rest of the oil and rosemary until hot; remove from heat. Grease a 9"x13" rectangular pan with some oil and pour in the batter. Squeeze the raisins to remove any water and sprinkle them along with the pine nuts on top. Pour the rosemary oil – without the leaves – over the surface. Bake in a 180°C/350°F preheated oven for about 45 minutes or until the top is well cracked and dark. Cooking time depends on the type of chestnut flour you used. Who knows why this simple and perfect dessert has such a disparaging name... perhaps due to its final aspect...! (Migliaccio or Castagnaccio. When the form –accio is added as a finale to an adjective in Italian, it implies negativity.)

MORSELLETTI SENESI
SIENESE NUT COOKIES
◆

1 1/4 cups sugar, 1/4 cup honey, 2 cups water, 11/2 cups flour, 2 teaspoons baking powder, 1/4 cup of each: chopped walnuts, chopped toasted almonds, chopped hazelnuts and chopped candied orange peel.

Put the sugar, honey and 2 cups of water in a saucepan and simmer until it becomes thickened syrup. Remove from heat and cool. In a large bowl, mix the flour and baking powder together. Pour in the syrup and mix vigorously with a wooden spoon. Add the chopped nuts and orange peel and mix. Set aside for

one hour. Flour a flat work surface; with your hands, break the dough into small pieces and form cylinders 2"x 1/2". Flatten them slightly and place them on a baking sheet lined with oven paper. Bake in a pre-heated 190°C/375°F oven for 20 minutes. Cool completely before serving with some good sweet wine like 'Passito'.

NECCI
CHESTNUT PANCAKES
◆

You will need two pizza stones for this recipe, 1 lb. chestnut flour, chestnut tree leaves, salt, 1 qt. water.

Mix the chestnut flour with the water in a bowl – being careful that the paste is not lumpy. The paste will be fluid and homogenous. You need to place the pizza stone in the oven; when hot cover the pizza stone with the chestnut leaves and pour a small amount of batter (about a tablespoon) on top. Cover the batter with other leaves and the second heated pizza stone. These cook quite quickly and are delicious served with fresh ricotta cheese. These are traditionally made using 'testi' which are pieces of either stone or terracotta. You can also use a pizza stone.

57

PALLE DI NEVE
SNOW BALLS
OR FLOATING ISLANDS
◆

1 qt. milk, 3 egg whites, pinch of salt, 1/4 cup powdered sugar.
<u>FOR THE CREAM</u>: *6 egg yolks, 1 cup sugar, 1/8 cup flour.*

Whip the egg whites to stiff peaks, slowly adding the salt and then the sugar. Boil the milk. When simmering, gently drop in tablespoons of the meringue and cook just until they float to the top. Be careful to only do one or two at a time. Set aside on a platter. Prepare the cream: beat the yolks, sugar and flour. Filter the milk that was used to cook the meringues and pour it into the cream base. Make sure the milk has cooled before proceeding. Cook the cream over low heat, stirring continuously with a wooden spoon until the top begins to thicken. Cool – almost completely – and pour it over the prepared snowballs. Serve with any type of cordial liqueur.

PAN DEI SANTI
SAINT'S BREAD

1 pound bread dough (Pasta di Pane, see recipe F), 3 tablespoons olive oil, 1 tablespoon honey, 1 cup of mixed dried chopped figs, chopped dates, pine nuts, raisins and walnuts, 1 egg yolk.

Using your hands, mix thoroughly all of the ingredients, except the yolk, into the bread dough.
Shape the dough into an oval shape and let it rest under a clean cloth until it has risen to twice its size. Roll the dough into an oval shape and brush the entire top of

the loaf with the egg yolk and place it on a greased baking sheet and bake it for roughly 45 minutes in a pre-heated 220°C/425°F oven. Serve cold. This dessert is traditionally served on All Saint's Day, November 1st.

PAN DI RAMERINO
ROSEMARY BUNS

FOR 8 TO 10 BUNS: 2 1/4 lbs. white flour, 1/2 oz. fresh compressed active beer yeast, 1 1/2 cups sugar, 1 cup warm water, 1 cup olive oil, 2 lbs. raisins, 1 stem fresh rosemary.

Mix the flour, yeast and sugar with the warm water and knead for several minutes. Form a ball and cover with a cloth and set aside to rest until doubled in size. Punch down dough and knead in the olive oil, raisins and some fresh rosemary (in Tuscany 'ramerino').

Knead the dough until all the ingredients are completely mixed. Divide the dough into small buns and place them on a baking sheet. Slash the tops with a sharp knife in the form of a cross.

Bake in a 200°C/400°F pre-heated oven until they're dark brown in color, about thirty minutes.

PANE PAZZO
OR PANE DI RADICOFANI
CRAZY BREAD

◆

1/2 oz. fresh compressed active beer yeast, 1 cup milk, just warmed, 3 cups flour, 1 tablespoon oil, 1/2 cup chestnut honey, 1 teaspoon whole black pepper corns, 1/4 cup raisins, plumped in hot water then squeezed to remove excess water.

Dissolve the dry yeast in the warm milk and pour it into the flour. Add the oil and knead with your hands until smooth and elastic. Cover with a cloth and let rise for about an hour. Flour a flat surface and begin kneading the dough and slowly adding the honey by spoonfuls, the pepper and raisins. Knead vigorously, adding flour to prevent the dough from sticking. Form the dough into a large loaf, cover it with a cloth and let it rest again for 1 hour. Then place it on a baking sheet. Bake in a 220°C/425°F pre-heated oven for 1 hour and 45 minutes. Cool before cutting into thick slices. This is excellent bread and great when accompanying game meats, given it's sweet-hot flavor.

PANETTONE FIORENTINO
FLORENTINE CANDIED FRUIT CAKE

◆

YOU MUST BEGIN THIS CAKE TWO DAYS BEFORE: 2 oz. fresh compressed active beer yeast, 1/2 cup milk

warm, 4 cups flour, 6 eggs, 1/2 cup mixed candied fruit: citron, orange peel, lemon peel, and cherries, 1/2 teaspoon powdered anise seed, 1/2 cup pine nuts, 1/4 cup raisins, 3/4 cup softened butter, 2 cups sugar, grated rind 1 lemon, 3 tablespoons powdered sugar.

Dissolve the yeast in the warm milk in a large bowl and add one-fourth of the flour. Knead until smooth and elastic. Place, covered with a cloth, in a warm place for 24 hours. Punch down the dough and knead in the rest of the flour. Briefly beat three of the eggs and add them to the dough.
Knead again until smooth and elastic. Place, covered with a cloth, in a warm place for another 24 hours. Punch down the dough and knead in the other ingredients: first the other 3 beaten eggs, candied fruit, raisins, pine nuts, anise seeds, the butter, sugar and, lastly, the grated lemon peel. Butter and flour a pan that is at least 10" round and 7" high (an Angel Food Pan without the hole) and cook for 1 hour in a pre-heated 180°C/350°F oven. Cool.
Delicately detach the cake from the sides of the pan using a flat spatula before turning out the cake. Dust with powdered sugar before serving.

61

PANFORTE DI SIENA
SIENESE FRUIT AND SPICE CAKE

◆

1/2 cup peeled almonds, 1/2 cup peeled hazelnuts, 1/4 cup cocoa powder (un-sweetened), 2 teaspoons cinnamon, 1/4 teaspoon each: cloves, nutmeg, coriander, 1/4 teaspoon ground vanilla bean, 1/4 cup flour, 1/2 cup each: candied citron, candied pumpkin, candied melon or orange peel, 1/3 cup sugar, 1/3 cup honey (millefiori), edible pastry paper, 1/4 cup powdered sugar.

Toast the almonds and hazelnuts in the oven. Remove and put them in a large bowl along with the cocoa powder, cinnamon, mixed spices, ground vanilla bean and the flour. Mix briefly.

Slice the candied fruit into small thin strips and add them as well. Set aside. In a small pot, melt the sugar and honey together. The syrup will become a whitish colored mass. It is ready when you remove a bit and with wet fingers can form a hard ball. Remove from heat and mix the sugar into the nut, fruit and spice mixture.

Mix vigorously for several minutes.

Line the bottom of a 10" spring-form pan with the edible patisserie paper and fill it with the mixture. Beat the pan on the counter to even out the batter.

Bake in pre-heated 160°C/325°F oven for 45 minutes. As soon as you remove the 'panforte' from the oven, open the spring-form and transfer the cake onto a platter. Dust with the powdered sugar only when completely cold.

Panforte is difficult to make because the recipe is elaborate and uses rich ingredients but it is highly satisfying once made and consumed.

PANFRITTO DOLCE
FRIED SWEET BREAD

◆

1 qt. milk, 1/2 teaspoon vanilla extract, 1 tablespoon powdered sugar, 4 slices day-old Italian bread (Tuscan un-salted), 1/4 cup flour, 2 eggs, beaten, 1/4 cup breadcrumbs, olive oil for frying.

To serve: apricot jam, cooked fruit: apples, pears and plums.

Mix the milk, vanilla and powdered sugar in a bowl. Slice the bread into small squares. Dip the squares in the milk, drip and roll in flour. Dip them in the beaten eggs, then roll in the breadcrumbs. Fry the bread pieces in hot oil, turning them until golden and crunchy.

Drain, then dry on absorbent paper. Prepare a tray: in the center place a small bowl of apricot jam or cooked mixed seasonal fruit.

Place the 'panfritto' all around and serve immediately. During wine harvest season 'panfritto' was made with wine must (partially fermented sweet grape juice)... instead of milk... these sweet cakes were really special then... eaten in the country and fried in giant pans one-after-another never-endingly by the housekeepers... how many we ate!

PANPEPATO
SPICED FRUIT CAKE

◆

1/2 cup honey, 1 cup sugar, 1 1/2 cups flour, 1/4 cup each: walnuts, hazelnuts, almonds, 1/8 cup each candied fruit: citron, melon, lemon peel, orange peel, 1/2 teaspoon coriander, 1/8 teaspoon each: cinnamon, hot pepper ('piper cubeba' or 'tellycherry' is the correct pepper you should use), cloves, nutmeg.

If you aren't using powdered spices, prepare the whole spices by grinding them finely in an electric grinder.

Put the honey and sugar in a large pot with a thick bottom and melt them, over a very low flame, stirring often with a wooden spoon. When the sugar turns a nice amber color, add the walnuts, hazelnuts and almonds. Mix briefly and remove from heat.

Pour into a large bowl. You must work quickly now so that the mixture doesn't solidify: stirring vigorously, add all of the flour at once. Next add the spices then the candied fruit, mixing well between each addition. Let rest for 5 minutes, always near the heat.

Pour batter into a low-sided 15" jelly-roll buttered pan, flour the top of the batter and bake in a pre-heated 190°C/375°F oven for twenty minutes.

As soon as you remove the cake from the oven, shake the pan to remove the flour topping. Let cool completely before serving or... it's even better the following day. A curiosity: legend says that you should add water and flame to the ingredients to make '17'... which has been the number of Siena's 'contrade' (districts) since long-ago 1675.

PAN SANTO *OR* PANE RICCO DEI CONTADINI
HOLY CAKES

◆

12 oz. day-old Italian bread, 2 cups milk, 2 eggs, beaten, 3 tablespoons sugar, oil for frying.

Heat a pan of frying oil to simmering. Slice the bread, not too thick, and dip it first in the milk then in the beaten eggs. Fry the prepared slices until golden. Drip and dry on absorbent paper.

Sprinkle the slices liberally with sugar and serve.

Traditionally, farmers would cook bread like this to use leftovers. They would also present it as a salty side-dish when sprinkled with salt and pepper instead of sugar.

This dish demonstrates how creative people became with day-old bread... a primary element of Tuscan cuisine.

PASTA REALE DEL GIOGO
ROYAL CAKE

◆

1 3/4 cups sugar, 5 eggs, separated, 2 2/3 cup flour, 3 tablespoons baking powder, grated rind of 1 lemon, butter.

Beat the egg whites to stiff peaks and set aside. Beat the egg yolks and sugar with a whisk in a large bowl. When light and thick, slowly add the flour and continue beating until blended.

Next the baking powder and grated lemon rind. Gently fold in the egg whites. Butter and flour a 9" round pan. Pour in the batter and bake in a pre-heated 190°C/375°F oven for 40 minutes. Cool completely before turning out. This cake is absolutely delicious just the way it is, but it is even better when sliced and filled with chocolate and vanilla pastry creams: cut the cake into three layers. Place the first disk on a serving tray and sprinkle with a mixture of Vin Santo and milk. Spread with prepared pastry cream then top with the second layer. Wet this layer and spread on prepared chocolate cream. Top with the last layer.

Dust the entire cake with powdered sugar and serve. In the humble homes of small villages located in the Appennino mountains (on the northern border of Tuscany and Emilia) this cake was made for important occasions such as weddings and served accompanied by piles of 'zuccherini' cookies that were made in different forms and variations. This was all presented to the happy couple as a gesture of good luck.

63

PATTONA
CHESTNUT POLENTA

◆

1 lb. chestnut flour, 1 qt. water, salt.

In a large pot, preferably copper, bring water and a bit of salt to boil.

Pour in the chestnut flour all at once and place a wooden spoon with a hole in the top in the center of the flour (known as 'Pattona') and as soon as boiling water comes out of the hole, begin stirring quickly, without stopping – clockwise so as to prevent lumps. Stir vigorously for about 30 minutes.

Stir the 'pattona' towards the center of the pot and try to un-stick the polenta from the side.

If you find that the polenta is not coming away easily, it requires further cooking. Pour the polenta out all at once, forming the classic shape of a pyramid. Serve hot or cold accompanied by fresh sweet ricotta or 'raveggiolo' cheese. To slice easily, use a piece of thick string.

PESCHE AL VINO ROSSO
PEACHES WITH RED WINE

◆

4 large, ripe yellow peaches, 1 cup red wine, 1/4 cup sugar, 1 whole clove, 1/2 teaspoon cinnamon.

Wash and peel the peaches and slice them into thin slices. Place them in a saucepan. Add the wine, water and spices. Cook over a low flame for 10 minutes. Put the peaches in a bowl, cool and set in the refrigerator at least an hour before serving.

These are delicious as an addition to a cream tart that's been decorated with fresh mint leaves.

PESCHE DI SEMOLINO GHIACCIATE
FROZEN PEACHES AND CREAM DESSERT

◆

4 ripe yellow peaches.

VANILLA SYRUP: 1/2 cup sugar, 2 cups water, 1 vanilla bean.

CREAM FILLING: 1 cup semolina, instant, 1 1/2 qts. milk, 1 cup sugar, 4 eggs, slightly beaten, 1/2 cup rum, 2 cups whipping cream.

Prepare the vanilla syrup: mix the sugar, water and vanilla bean in a medium pan and bring to a boil; then lower the heat. Wash the peaches and cut them in half and remove the pit.

Put them in the syrup and cook them for several minutes, making sure that they stay whole.

Remove the peaches from the syrup, drain and place them on a serving tray. Remove the vanilla bean from the syrup and pour it into a serving bowl to cool. Prepare the cream filling: bring the milk and sugar to a boil; remove from heat and add the semolina slowly, while whisking continuously. Cool slightly. Add the eggs and the rum. Mix well and set aside to cool completely. Whip the cream until stiff and gently fold it into the semolina mixture.

Using an ice-cream scoop (or a simple spoon), scoop the filling by balls around the peaches that are on the tray. Place the tray either in the freezer or refrigerator for at least an hour before serving. Serve with the reserved vanilla syrup.

PICCOLE FOGLIE D'ALLORO
LAUREL LEAF COOKIES

<u>RECIPE FOR ABOUT 25 COOKIES</u>: 1 cup flour, 2 table-spoons softened butter, 4 egg yolks + 1 white, 1/4 cup sugar, pinch of salt, 2 tablespoons milk, laurel leaves.

Sift the flour into a mound on a flat work surface. Add the butter, egg yolks, sugar and salt. Knead energetically. Knead in the milk. When the dough is smooth, roll it out to 1/4-inch high. Using a laurel leaf as a guide, cut the cookies out with a sharp knife and place them on a baking sheet lined with oven paper.
Briefly whisk the egg white and brush it on each leaf. Bake in a 190°C/375°F pre-heated oven for 20 minutes. Variation: dip the leaf cookies in melted dark chocolate. Refrigerate them for at least an hour before serving.

PINOCCATE DELLA VAL DI CHIANA
VAL DI CHIANA PINE NUT CANDIES
◆

2 cups sugar, 1 cup pine nuts, 1/2 cup dark cocoa powder (non sugared), 1 tablespoon flour, grated peel 1 lemon.

Cook the sugar and one cup of water in a pot over a moderate flame stirring constantly until thick and syrupy. Remove from flame and add the pine nuts, cocoa powder and flour; mix. Add the grated peel. Pour the candy onto a floured surface. Working quickly, roll the candy with a wet rolling pin to 1/2-inch. Cool. Cut into rectangles using a sharp knife. Wrap each piece individually with waxed paper and store in a hermetically sealed jar.

PINOCCHIATA
PINE NUT BRITTLE

◆

1 cup pine nuts, 1 cup sugar, 1 cup red wine, 4 whole cloves, olive oil.

Melt the sugar in a medium saucepan over low heat. Stir frequently by rotating the pot by the handle. Once melted, add the pine nuts, wine and cloves.

Continue rotating the pot until the sugar is nicely caramelized - fluid and homogeneous (candy thermometer reading 135°C/275°F).

Lightly oil a flat (non wooden) surface (like marble as it should be cold) and pour the mixture evenly on top.

Let cool and break with a large knife into different shapes.

A simpler version of classic brittle but with a special touch... red wine!

PINOCCHIATI DI PISTOIA
PISTOIA PINE NUT CANDIES

◆

1 1/4 cups sugar, 1 cup pine nuts, 1 cup water, 1 teaspoon vanilla extract, candy paper cups (pirottini).

Put the sugar in a pot over low flame and, using a wooden spoon, stir in the water a little at a time.

Boil for about 15 minutes until it becomes thickened syrup.

Now, put the syrup pot over another pot of simmering hot water.

Add the pine nuts.

Continue cooking, stirring continuously, until the sugar becomes a white glaze. Stir in the vanilla extract and continue cooking another 10 minutes.

Portion the candy into individual candy paper cups using a teaspoon. Cool before serving. These are delicious in the summer served with iced coffee.

POLENTA DOLCE ALL'ARETINA
SWEET POLENTA AREZZO STYLE

◆

1 1/2 qts. water, pinch of salt, 2 1/2 cups chestnut flour, 1 cup fresh ricotta cheese.

Bring the water to a boil in a large pot. Add salt. Remove the pot from the heat and slowly pour in the chestnut flour. Put the pot back over a medium-low flame and cook, stirring constantly for 45 minutes until done (check package for time). When cooked, pour the polenta out onto a flat serving dish and serve hot with fresh ricotta cheese – perhaps with a little sugar added. This dish is also excellent served cold, cut into large slices that have been toasted on a grill.

POPPE DI MONACA
EGG MOUNDS

◆

2 1/2 cups sugar, 6 egg yolks, softened butter.

Whip the sugar and yolks together until they become pale and dense. Brush the softened butter on a baking sheet so that it's distributed evenly. Spoon 'mounds' onto the prepared sheet; making sure that they're not too close together. Bake for 15 minutes in a pre-heated 200°C/400°F oven.

Remove them from the oven before they change color. Serve while still warm and mushy. These 'poppe' are not to be confused with 'africani' that are cooked in candy papers and are characteristically brown in color.

QUARESIMALI
LENT ALPHABET COOKIES

◆

3/4 cup flour, 3/4 cup powdered sugar, 1/4 cup powdered dark un-sweetened cocoa powder, 1 egg + 1 white.

Beat the egg and egg white with the sugar until thick and foamy. Add the flour and cocoa and beat for several minutes. Prepare a baking sheet by buttering it. Put the batter into a large pastry bag, fitted with a medium round tip, and squeeze out letters (any you like) onto a greased sheet. They should be about 1 1/2-inchs in length.

Bake in a pre-heated 160°C/325°F oven for 15 minutes. During Lent these simple cookies were once made in abundance and presented mounded on trays in many Florentine bakeries. Because they're so easy to make, try them for a child's afternoon snack or fill cellophane bags and tie them with colored ribbons to present as a token gift of good wishes.

RAVIOLI DOLCI DEL CASENTINO
CASENTINO SWEET RAVIOLI

<u>DOUGH</u>: *1 1/2 cups flour, 2 eggs, water.*
<u>FILLING</u>: *3 eggs, 1 lb. fresh ricotta cheese, 6 tablespoons sugar, olive oil for frying.*

Pour the flour onto a flat work surface and add 2 of the eggs, blending with your hands. If necessary, add some cold water so that the dough is smooth. Form a ball, cover and set aside for 1 hour. Prepare the filling: Mix the eggs, ricotta

67

cheese and sugar in a bowl. On a floured surface roll out the prepared pasta dough to a long strip that is 4 inches wide. Spoon the filling in mounds onto half of the strip of dough, spacing well. Fold the other half of dough over the top and press down gently between each mound to seal them.

Cut the ravioli out with a sharp knife or a zigzag rolling cutter. In a large pan, bring the frying oil to a boil. Gently put in the ravioli, turning them during frying and cook until golden. Remove, drip and dry on absorbent paper. Dust immediately with sugar. Serve cold.

RICCIARELLI DI SIENA
RICCIARELLI ALMOND COOKIES
◆

FOR 20 RICCIARELLI: *20 edible pastry papers ('carta ostie'), 1cup sweet peeled almonds, 1/4 cup bitter peeled almonds, 1 1/4 cup sugar, 2 egg whites, grated rind 1 orange.*

Prepare the edible paper: place the 'ricciarello' oblong cutter on the paper and cut out 20 shapes using a sharp knife. Set aside. (Ricciarelli's have a very noteworthy shape – oblong. If you don't have the original cutter, you may use any oblong shaped cutter).

Finely grind the almonds using a mortar and pestle (or a modern electric grinder if you prefer), adding 2 tablespoons of sugar at a time. When done grinding, add the rest of the sugar and mix. Whip the egg whites to a stiff peak and add the orange peel. Fold in the almonds mixture a bit at a time.

Flour a flat working surface and wet a rolling pin with cold water. Gently roll out the mixture to a height of 1/2-inch.

Cut out 20 cookies with the oblong cutter and gently set them on top of the prepared papers and set on a baking sheet. Bake in a pre-heated 160°C/325°F oven for 45 minutes. Serve cold sprinkled liberally with powdered sugar.

ROSCHETTE
DONUT COOKIES
◆

2 1/2 cups flour, 2 cups cold water, 3 tablespoons oil, 1/2 cup sugar, 2 teaspoons salt.

Mix the flour, oil and cold water together and turn it out on to a floured work surface and knead until smooth and solid. Cover with a damp cloth and let rest for 30 minutes. Break pieces of the dough off and form small cylinders that you'll then form into donuts. Continue until all of the dough has been used. Place the donuts on a baking sheet lined with oven paper. Sprinkle half of the cookies with sugar and the other half with salt. Bake for 30 minutes in a 160°C/325°F preheated oven until golden and crunchy. Serve when completely cooled. As a fun snack/toy for the children: hang them from a cotton cord that the children can wear around their necks. This tradition was introduced to Livorno when the first Portuguese Jews (Ebrei Lusitani) came around the mid-1800's.

ROVENTINI ALL'USO DI SIENA
PIG'S BLOOD FRITTERS
◆

2 cups fresh pig's blood, 1 qt. water, 1 cup milk, 2 cups chopped Cavallucci cookies (see recipe Cavallucci), 1 slice day-old Italian bread (Tuscan style un-salted), pinch grated nutmeg, 1 lemon peel, 1/2 cup Vin Santo wine, 6 eggs, 4 tablespoons sugar, 1/2 cup flour, olive oil for frying.

Strain the pig's blood (found only through special order) through a fine sieve. Mix the blood with the quart of water and set aside.

In a large pot, briefly cook the milk, crumbled Cavallucci cookies and the bread. Remove from heat and add the nutmeg, lemon peel and Vin Santo wine. Set aside for 10 minutes then pass through a sieve. Mix this liquid with the blood.

Set aside. In a large bowl beat the eggs, sugar and flour. Add the blood and bread mixture and blend until just barely mixed. Heat a pan with frying oil and drop 1/4-cup sized dollops into it. Fry both sides.

Drip and dry well on absorbent paper. You'll want to dry them additionally by placing some absorbent paper on top as well. Serve hot and sprinkled with sugar.

SALAME DOLCE
SWEET SALAME LOG

1 1/2 cups non-egg made cookie crumbs (any type of simple dry vanilla cookie will do), 3/4 cup sugar, 11/8 cup softened butter, 1/2 cup pine nuts - chopped, 2 tablespoons cocoa powder (non-sugared), 1/4 cup Vin Santo wine.

Melt the butter and put aside to cool. Prepare the cookie crumbs and mix them in a bowl with the cooled butter, sugar, cocoa powder, chopped pine nuts and Vin Santo. Mix well, even using hands, and form into a salame. Wrap the log in aluminum or waxed paper as tightly as possible. Refrigerate several hours. Serve only when cold by cutting it into large slices.

This is a favorite snack among children (and not only!). It reflects the age-old art of using leftovers to produce delicious treats. How can I say this... it's not necessary to use rich ingredients to make a party.

The spirit of our land is that it is varied and perfect... even if little remains in the larder, you can still give joy to the cook as well as those who eat it. You can see this in our boiled meat hashes ('lesso rifatto') or bread gnocchi ('gnocchetti di pane raffermo')... or 'salame dolce'.

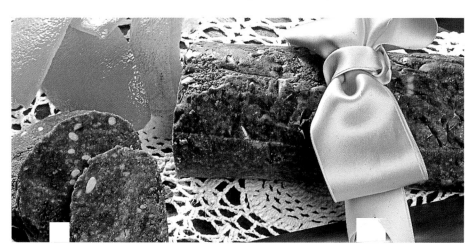

SAPA DELL'ARETINO
THISTLE AND QUINCE APPLES

◆

RECIPE FOR 4 TO 5 1/2 CUP JARS: 1 qt. cooked wine must, 5 quince apples, 6 thistle stalks, found as specialty in fruit & vegetable markets ('cardi'), 1 1/2 cup chopped walnuts, 1 cup sugar.

Pour the wine must, apples and chopped thistle stalks in a large pot. Cook over low heat for 1 1/2 hours, stirring often with a wooden spoon. Add the sugar, chopped nuts and cook another hour. Cool the 'sapa' and pour it into jam jars. Around Arezzo, 'sapa' is made like this, with quince apples and thistle that are typically found in autumn. In other areas of Tuscany, such as the Appennino Tosco-Emiliano mountains, 'sapa' is prepared with other fruit but always with wine must.

SCHIACCIA PASQUALE
EASTER BREAD

📷

4 1/2 cups flour, 2 teaspoons active dry beer yeast, 2 tablespoons olive oil, 1 teaspoon ground anise seeds, 1/2 cup raisins, plumped in hot water and squeezed dry, 1/2 cup Vin Santo wine, 5 eggs, 1 cup sugar, 1/4 cup lard, 1 egg yolk.

On a floured work surface mound the flour, the yeast and add the olive oil, anise and Vin Santo. Knead until just mixed. In a bowl mix the eggs and sugar then pour them into the flour. Add the raisins and lastly, the lard. Knead, adding flour when the dough gets sticky, until elastic and smooth. Set aside, covered by a cloth for 24 hours. Punch down and knead again for several minutes. Divide the dough in two parts, set them aside for an hour. Butter and flour a baking sheet and place the 'schiaccie' on it (a funny name for these bread rolls) and brush the tops with the beaten egg yolk. Bake in a pre-heated 160°C/325°F oven for 1 hour. It is traditional to make two loaves because it represents a 'donation' made on Easter morning. Women in the country would prepare a many of these loaves and then 'donate' them to relatives and friends for Easter.

SCHIACCIATA ALLA FIORENTINA
FLORENTINE MARDI GRAS CAKE

1 oz. fresh compressed active beer yeast (dissolved in 3 tablespoons warm water), 2 1/2 cups flour, 1 1/4 cups lard, 3/4 cup sugar, 4 eggs, grated peel (only orange part) 1 orange, pinch of salt, powdered sugar.

Place the prepared yeast in a bowl with the flour. Mix, using a wooden spoon, until smooth. Let rest for about an hour until doubled in volume. Knead well and slowly add the sugar, eggs, 1 cup of the lard, a pinch of salt and the grated or-ange rind. Knead the dough for several minutes until smooth. Grease a 9"x13" rectangular pan with the remaining lard, fill with dough and let rise in a dry place for about 2 hours. Bake in a pre-heated 190°C/375°F oven for 30 minutes. Check with a toothpick for doneness. Once cooled, dust liberally with pow-dered sugar. The secret of this recipe is the levitation that takes place twice and the quality lard used. Don't be tempted, as often happens these days, to fill the center with creams – I've even seen them filled with chocolate mousse! Original 'schiacciata alla fiorentina' is eaten like this: simple, perfect, light and flavorful.

SFORMATO CON ZABAIONE
CREAM SOUFFLÉ WITH ZABAIONE

◆

<u>FOR THE CREAM</u>: *2 eggs, 2 tablespoons sugar, 1 cup milk, boiled, 1 vanilla bean.*
<u>FOR THE ZABAIONE</u>: *2 egg yolks, 3 tablespoons Marsala wine, 2 tablespoons sugar.*
<u>FOR THE SOUFFLÉ</u>: *1 package lady finger cookies (you need about 25), 1 cup Marsala wine, 1/2 cup sultana raisins, plumped in hot water then squeezed to remove excess water, 1/4 cup mixed chopped candied fruit, butter.*

Prepare the cream: beat the egg yolks and sugar with a whisk in a small pot. Put the pot over another larger pot of hot water and start cooking. Slowly pour in the boiled milk and then add the vanilla bean. Cook for about 10 minutes and remove from heat. Discard the vanilla bean. Set aside. Prepare the Soufflé: butter a 81/2" ring pan. Dip the ladyfingers in the marsala wine – be careful not to wet them too much or they'll break – and line the ring with them.
Sprinkle the cookies with the raisins and candied fruit. (If your guests include children or adults who don't like liqueurs, you can substitute the Marsala with sugared orange juice). Pour the cream on top and place the ring in a larger pan filled with hot water and bake in a pre-heated oven 180°C/350°F for 45 minutes.
In the meantime, prepare the zabaione: Beat the egg yolks, adding the sugar and then the marsala a drop at a time. Beat until smooth, thick and creamy. Remove the soufflé from the oven, turn it - without removing the pan - onto a serving platter and cool completely. Serve with the zabaione cream poured into the center of the ring.

SOMMOMMOLI
RAISIN FRITTERS

◆

1 cup flour, 3 teaspoons active dry beer yeast, 3 egg yolks, 1/2 cup sugar, 1/4 cup raisins, plumped in hot water then squeezed to remove excess water, grated peel of 1 orange, oil for frying.

Mix the flour and yeast together and add a cup of water. Stir with a wooden spoon to form a dense, smooth dough. In another bowl whisk the egg yolks with half the sugar and add them to the flour mix. Add the orange peel and the plumped raisins. Set aside for one hour. Heat some frying oil in a large pan and bring it to a boil. Slowly drop in tablespoonfuls of the batter. Turn during cooking and fry to golden. Drip-drain and dry on absorbent paper. Sprinkle the remaining sugar on top and serve while still hot. The funny name 'Sommommolo" comes from the lumpy aspect of these fritters – they look like a closed fist that in the Florentine quarter of San Frediano is known as a 'sommommolo'... or rather, a fist coming up to meet a chin.

SORBETTO ARANCIA ALLA CATERINA DE' MEDICI
CATHERINE DE MEDICI'S ORANGE SORBET

2.2 lbs. non-treated oranges, 1 3/4 cups sugar, 2 cups water, 1 lemon, 5 drops orange blossom extract, 1 teaspoon vanilla extract, 1 egg white.

Wash the oranges. Peel two oranges with a potato peeler.

Cut the peel into thin slices and put them in a saucepan together with a little water. Boil for about 3 minutes, drain and rinse.

Repeat the process, boiling the strips of orange peel for another 5 minutes. Set aside. Make syrup with 1 1/2 cups of the sugar and two cups of water.

Boil until it starts to foam on the surface. Remove from heat and add the cooked orange peel. Set aside to marinate for one hour. Squeeze the remaining oranges and the lemon. Strain the juice.

Add the orange blossom water. Strain the sugar syrup to remove the peel and add to the juice.

Pour the mixture into an ice-cream maker and start the process.

Make another syrup with the remaining 1/4 cup of sugar, 2 tablespoons of water and add the vanilla extract.

Cool. Beat the egg white to stiff peaks. Add the syrup drop-by-drop until a stiff, shiny mixture is formed.

When the sorbet begins thickening, add the meringue one spoon at a time and finish the creaming process.

For an equally delightful variation, you can make lemon sorbet by substituting un-treated lemons for the oranges. Organic fruit, now available everywhere, is unmistakable in perfume and flavor; there is no substitute for it.

73

SORBETTO DI FRAGOLINE DI BOSCO
WILD STRAWBERRY SORBET

◆

1 1/2 lbs. wild strawberries, 1 1/4 cups sugar, 2 qt. water, juice of 1/2 lemon, 1 egg white, white wine.

Wash the strawberries with the white wine and puree them in a blender. Prepare syrup: pour 1 cup of the sugar into 2 quarts of water and cook over a moderate flame. When bubbles start to form on the surface, remove and cool slightly. Add the strawberry puree and the lemon juice. Pour the mixture into an ice-cream machine and start the process. Melt the remaining sugar with 2 tablespoons of water in a small saucepan. Set aside. Beat the egg white to a stiff peak and slowly drizzle the sugar water into it. Beat until the consistency is thick and shiny. Slowly put spoonfuls of the whites into the thickening sorbet and finish the ice-cream program. Serve with some wild strawberries and fresh mint leaves for garnish. If you don't have an ice-cream maker: don't despair! Pour the strawberry puree into any freezer-safe container and freeze, stirring every once in a while as it thickens. Slowly add the meringue mixture with a whisk. Freeze 45 minutes and enjoy!

SORBETTO DI SALVIA AL VIN BIANCO
SAGE AND WHITE WINE SORBET

◆

1 cup fresh sage leaves, 1 cup water, 1 cup sugar, strained juice of 1 lemon, 3 cups white wine, 1 egg white.

Carefully wash and dry the fresh sage leaves and put them into a saucepan with a cup of water and the sugar.
Boil over a low flame until the sugar begins to bubble. Add the lemon juice and white wine. Mix well and set aside to marinade for 1 hour before pouring it into an ice-cream maker. Start the processor. Beat the egg white into stiff peaks and when the sorbet is just thickened fold it into the mixture. Continue the process until the sorbet is ready. This sorbet is ideal as light course in the middle of a rich luncheon or dinner, especially when dining on game meats.

STIACCIATA (SCHIACCIATA CON L'UVA)
GRAPE SWEET BREAD

📷

The grapes used in this recipe are commonly found in most markets and/or supermarkets in Italy during grape harvest in September and October. You may substitute them with any small, dark wine grape.
1 stem rosemary + some extra for topping, 1 pound bread dough (Pasta di pane, see recipe G), 2 pounds black wine grapes, washed with stems removed (sangiovese grapes), 5 tablespoons sugar, 1 cup red wine, 2 tablespoons olive oil.

Heat the rosemary and olive oil in a small pan. Remove the rosemary as soon as the oil is heated. Cool slightly. Knead the prepared bread dough with the rosemary oil until it is totally absorbed. Spread half of the dough in the bottom of an oiled 9"x 13" baking sheet. Squeeze the grapes slightly and put almost all of them

onto the prepared dough (use only small grapes). Sprinkle with 3 tablespoons of sugar. Cover the grapes with the other half of the dough. Put the remaining grapes on top and press them slightly into the dough. Sprinkle with the remaining sugar, some fresh rosemary. Pour the red wine evenly over the top. Bake in a pre-heated 190°C/375°F oven for about 30 minutes or until golden brown. Serve cold.

At the end of September the countryside is hot and sunny like Tuscany. It's the moment that the golden orioles sit resting in the tall lime trees before migrating towards warmer climes.

Here in Pulkau, a small village in far-eastern Austria, time moves slowly and is noticed only by the striking of the clock in the town square's tower. Friends of the Nebehay, the family of long-time booksellers whom I visit every summer, will arrive in the afternoon to play some music and taste some typ-ical Italian desserts. I breathe deeply while sitting under a mulberry tree in the garden. All at once I know what I'll prepare for them: la schiacciata con l'uva. In the distance I hear the rumble of tractors tilling the earth. The sweet odor of dirt is mixed with the perfume of flowers. It's the perfect setting for serving a dessert that is prepared with rural and wine harvest ingredients. I prepare the bread dough quickly so that it may rise and flatten it out onto a greased sheet. This kitchen is so modern and organized... with its straw braid of vegetables (bought at the open market Loggia del Porcellino) from Florence. It's a perfect marriage of colors with the dark grapes I'm mashing. I'm so happy while pressing the last grapes onto the 'schiacciata' and placing it in the ultra-modern oven. However, something is missing. It's not completely perfect. My brain feverishly tries in vain to recall what isn't quite right... there it is... it's the smell, the perfume! Here in Pulkau they don't even know what rosemary is!

STIACCIATA UNTA
SWEET PORK FOCACCIA

◆

This is one of the recipes that you may find hard to make as it requires 'ciccioli', that is, dried, salted and flaked pork rind.

1 1/2 lbs. bread dough (Pasta di pane, see recipe G), 1/2 cup sugar, 5 egg yolks, 8 oz. chopped ciccioli, pinch of salt, grated peel of 1 orange, 2/3 cup lard, powdered sugar.

Slowly knead the prepared bread dough. Add the sugar, 4 beaten egg yolks, pork shavings, salt, grated peel, and lastly, all but 3 tablespoons of the lard. Using floured hands form a ball and cover it with a cloth. Let rise for at least an hour. Punch down the dough and knead in the beaten yolks and the remaining lard. Oil a 9 x 13" rectangular baking pan and fill it with the risen dough. Bake in a pre-heated oven 200°C/400°F for about 45 minutes. When baked, remove from pan and cool. Sprinkle with powdered sugar.

TORCOLO
MIXED FRUIT RING CAKE

◆

1 cup pine nuts, 2 3/4 cups flour, 1/8 teaspoon baking soda, 1/4 cup sultana raisins, 1 cup sugar, 1 egg, 1/3 cup softened butter, pinch of anise seeds, 1/2 cup mixed chopped candied fruit.

Toast the pine nuts and grind them finely. Put the flour and baking soda on a flat work surface. Working with your hands, add the ground

nuts, plumped raisins, sugar, egg and butter. Mix well. Add the anise seeds and candied fruit. Knead the dough several minutes until smooth and elastic. Form a large ring with the dough and place it on a greased and lightly floured baking sheet. Bake in a preheated 190°C/375°F oven for 45 minutes. Cool completely before serving in thick slices.

TORTA COI BECCHI
SPINACH, CHARD AND RICOTTA TART

◆

1 recipe pastry dough (Pasta frolla, see recipe C), 2 bunches fresh spinach, washed carefully, 1 bunch fresh Swiss chard, washed carefully, 2 eggs, 3/4 cup sugar, 8 oz. fresh ricotta cheese, 1/4 cup raisins, plumped in hot water then squeezed to remove excess water, 1 yolk, beaten.

Prepare the pastry dough and set it aside. In a pot with a little water cook the spinach and chard. Drain and squeeze out the water. Beat the eggs and sugar in a large bowl and add the ricotta and raisins a little at a time. Chop the spinach and chard coarsely and add them to the mixture. Roll out the prepared dough to 1/4-inch thick and line a buttered and floured 9" cake pan, leaving the dough to overhang the edge. Pour in the batter and pinch and crimp the dough on the edge of the pan. The crimped edge is called 'becchi', which is where this pie gets its name. Brush the egg yolk on top. Place in a 190°C/375°F pre-heated oven and bake for 45 minutes.

TORTA COI BISCHERI
CHOCOLATE AND RICE CAKE

Pastry dough (Pasta frolla, see recipe C), 3 cups milk, 1/2 cup sugar, 1/2 teaspoon salt, 2/3 cup white rice (Arborio), 1/8 cup raisins, 1/3 cup chopped mixed candied fruits, grated peel 1 lemon, 1/2 cup grated dark chocolate, 1 egg white, powdered sugar to garnish.

Prepare the pastry dough and set it aside. Boil the milk, sugar and salt together. Add the rice, stir often and lower the flame as much as possible. When all of the liquid is absorbed and the rice is cooked, remove it from the heat. Mix in the raisins, candied fruits, grated lemon peel and lastly, the grated dark chocolate. Roll out the prepared pastry dough (no higher than 1/4-inch) and place it in a buttered and floured 9" springform; let the dough hang over the sides as you'll need to fold over the edges later. Fill the pastry dough with the prepared rice filling. Fold over the over-hanging dough. It doesn't matter if it doesn't reach the center and the top isn't completely covered. Briefly beat the egg white with a fork and brush the top of the dough. Bake in a pre-heated 220°C/425°F oven for 45 minutes. The tart is cooked when golden. Dust with powdered sugar when cold. The word 'bischeri', typically Tuscan, is often used to express disdain or stupidity; however it shouldn't only be thought of that way.

The Bischeri were a noble family dating back to the Florentine Renaissance period. There is still a street with their name on it. The noun Bischeri developed into a substantive verb due to the family's not-too-brilliant history!

77

TORTA DEI CERTOSINI
CERTOSINI CAKE

1/4 cup each: dried figs, raisins, 3/4 cup each: peeled almonds, hazelnuts, 2 1/2 cups flour, 2 teaspoons baking powder, 2/3 cup honey, 1/2 cup sugar, 2 eggs, pinch of cinnamon, 1/4 teaspoon vanilla extract, 1/4 cup candied orange, chopped finely, 1/4 cup butter, softened, milk, 1/4 cup grappa liqueur (or Liquore dei Certosini).

Put the chopped almonds, hazelnuts and figs in a bowl. Set aside. Mound the flour on a flat surface and mix in the baking powder.

Form a crater in the center and put in the prepared nuts and figs, honey and plumped raisins. Start kneading, flouring the hands as needed.

At this point, place the dough in a bowl and add the beaten eggs, cinnamon and vanilla.

Blend the dough with this ingredients, using a wooden spoon and set aside for 30 minutes.

Stir well and mix in the butter, liqueur, orange peel and just enough milk to form a smooth batter.

Put the batter into a 9" x 13" rectangular pan with low sides.

Let rest 10 minutes before baking in a 190°C/375°F pre-heated oven for 45 minutes.

Test by inserting a toothpick; it should come out clean.

Turn out the cake only when it is completely cooled, to keep the surface from cracking.

Torta di Farro e Ricotta
Spelt Wheat and Ricotta Cake

2/3 cup spelt wheat, 2 qts. milk, 3 tablespoons sugar, 2 teaspoons cinnamon, 2 teaspoons vanilla, 4 eggs, separated, 1/2 cup spelt wheat flour (can be substituted with white flour), 1 cup fresh ricotta cheese, 3/4 cup raisins, plumped in hot water then squeezed to remove water, grated rind of 1 lemon, pinch of salt, 1/2 cup orange liqueur (Rosolio di arancia).

Mix the spelt wheat, milk, sugar, cinnamon and vanilla together in a large pot and cook – over a low flame – according to wheat package directions. (I suggest you follow the package directions because several different types of spelt wheat exist and they could have been treated differently and have different cooking times.) Mix often while cooking. Cool slightly. Beat the egg yolks with the spelt flour, ricotta, raisins, grated lemon peel and pinch of salt. Blend into the cooked wheat. Cool completely. Beat the egg whites and fold into the cooled batter. Butter a 2-quart baking dish and pour in the batter. Bake in a preheated 180°C/350°F oven for 45 minutes.

Test to see if a toothpick comes out clean. Unmold and pour the orange liqueur on top. Serve either hot or cold.

TORTA DI MELE
APPLE CAKE
📷

5 tart apples, juice of 1 lemon, 1/2 cup flour, 2 tea-spoons baking powder, 1 1/2 cups sugar, 2 eggs, 1/2 cup softened butter, 1 cup milk.

Peel and slice the apples into thin slices and place them in a bowl. Sprinkle the slices with the juice of one lemon and stir it gently to prevent the slices from turning brown.

In a medium bowl, mix all of the other ingredients and blend thoroughly. Fold in the apple slices.

Butter a 8" square pan and pour in the batter. Sprinkle the top with sugar. Bake in a pre-heated 180°C/350 °F oven for forty minutes. Check doneness with a toothpick.

This simple cake was made in the kitchen of my youth. Most often it was made with wild apples – red, tart and hard. Their perfume filled the house. We'd be called in from the garden where we'd be playing to eat it accompanied by glasses of warm milk.

TORTA DI PANE E AMARETTI
BREAD AND AMARETTO PUDDING
◆

2 lbs. day-old Italian bread (if you can find Tuscan-style unsalted bread use that), 1 qt. whole milk, 1/4 cup sugar, 1 cup crumbled amaretto cookies, 1/4 cup sultana raisins, plumped in hot water than squeezed to remove excess water, butter and bread crumbs.

Slice the bread and place it in a large bowl with the milk. When the milk is completely absorbed, add the crumbled amaretto cookies, sugar, slightly beaten yolks and plumped raisins. Mix well until completely blended and the bread is totally broken-up.

Set aside for 15 minutes. Beat the egg whites until they form peaks and fold them gently into the bread. Butter and bread-crumb a 2-quart shallow baking dish and pour in the batter; bake in pre-heated 220°C/425°F oven for 45 minutes. The dessert is ready when the surface is crunchy and golden. Serve with a sprinkling of powdered sugar.

TORTA DOLCE DI PROSEZZO
PROSEZZO POTATO CAKE
◆

2.2 lbs. potatoes (mashing type), 1/2 cup flour, 2 eggs, 1/2 cup sugar, 1/4 cup softened butter, 1/4 scant cup raisins, plumped in hot water then squeezed to remove excess water, 1 tablespoon candied orange peel, chopped finely, 2 teaspoons baking powder, 1/2 cup milk.

Boil the potatoes, peel and mash them well. Whisk the eggs and sugar together and add them, the flour and the butter to the potatoes. Mix well. Add the raisins and candied orange and mix.

Heat the milk to warm and dissolve the baking powder in it. Add the liquid to the potato mixture and mix only until just blended. Set aside for 30 minutes. Pour the batter into a buttered 9"round pan

and bake in a pre-heated 190°C/375°F oven for 30 minutes. Turn out the cake by gently tapping the sides to loosen it and only when cool.

TORTA "LA BIANCA" DI PRATO
WHITE CAKE – PRATO STYLE

◆

10 egg whites, 1 1/2 cups sugar, 1/2 cup butter, 1/3 cup sifted flour, 1/2 cup potato flour, finely grated peel 1 lemon, 1/2 cup chopped almonds, 1/4 cup powdered sugar.

Melt the butter and cool slightly. Beat the egg whites, slowly adding the sugar by spoonfuls; when they almost form stiff peaks, slowly add the flour, potato flour and lemon peel. While beating, add the melted butter. Heavily butter a 9" round baking pan and press the chopped almonds into the bottom so that they stick. Pour in the batter, making sure that it is even in the pan. Bake in a pre-heated 160°C/325°F oven for about 1 hour. Cool completely before turning out. If you turn it out too soon, the cake will break.

Dust the top with the powdered sugar, which will give the cake the white appearance from which it gets its name.

TORTA PISANA DI MANDORLE
PISA STYLE ALMOND CAKE

◆

1/3 cup sweet peeled almonds, 1/8 cup bitter almonds, 1 1/2 cups sugar, 2/3 cup flour, 9 eggs - separated, grated rind 1 lemon, 1/4 cup powdered sugar.

Toast the almonds and then grind them finely. Put them in a bowl with the flour and 1 tablespoon of the sugar and mix briefly. Set aside. Beat the egg yolks with the rest of the sugar and then add the flour mixture. Beat until well mixed. Beat the egg whites and lemon peel until they form stiff peaks. Fold into the yolk mixture. Pour batter into a buttered and floured 10" round pan and bake in a pre-heated 190°C/375°F oven for 45 minutes. Test for doneness with a toothpick. Turn the hot cake out onto a serving dish and cool for at least 30 minutes before dusting with powdered sugar.

VINATA DI FARRO
SPELT WHEAT PUDDING

◆

3/4 cup spelt wheat, 1 qt. grape must (may be substituted with grape juice), 1 cup granulated brown sugar, 3 tablespoons gelatin.
Soak the spelt wheat in the grape must over night. Cook the wheat over low heat in the liquid it was soaked in according to package directions. Stir in the sugar and gelatin. Set aside for about 30 minutes. Pour the pudding into a buttered 1-qt. mold and refrigerate at least 3-4 hours before serving. Serve with cold lightly whipped cream.

ZUCCHERINI DI FIRENZUOLA
SUGAR COOKIES –
FIRENZUOLA STYLE

4 3/4 cups white flour, 8 eggs, 1/2 cup softened butter, 1 cup sugar, 1 teaspoon vanilla extract, 4 teaspoons baking powder, anise seeds, 1 1/2 cup powdered sugar, 1/2 cup Alkermes liqueur.

Prepare the dough as for "Vernio Sugar Cookies". Form the cookies by dividing the dough into four rolls. Roll out each ball to finger height long tubes. Flatten the tops and cut the dough into diagonal slices. Place each oblique strip on a buttered baking sheet and bake in a preheated 180°C/350°F oven for 20 minutes. Cool completely. When cool, wet the powdered sugar with the Alkermes liqueur and dip each cookie. Dredge each cookie completely in the sugar and drip-dry on a cooling rack.

ZUCCHERINI DI VERNIO
SUGAR COOKIES - VERNIO STYLE

4 3/4 cups white flour, 8 eggs, 1 cup sugar, 1/2 cup softened butter, 4 teaspoons baking powder, 1 teaspoon vanilla extract, 1/2 teaspoon anise seeds, a light sprinkle of Anisette liqueur, 1 1/2 cup powdered sugar.

Mound the flour on work surface and break the eggs in the center. Add the sugar and the butter. Knead gently and add, one at a time, the baking powder, vanilla, anise seeds. Sprinkle with some Anisette liqueur. Form a ball and set aside for about 30 minutes. Make the cookies by pinching off the dough

and forming little doughnuts in the palm of your hand; rings should be about finger size but not too wide. Set them on a greased baking sheet and bake for about 20 minutes in a preheated 180°C/350°F oven. Cool completely. In a pan over simmering water, dissolve the powdered sugar with a few drops of cold water. Dunk the cooled cookies into the sugar paste to cover them well and put them aside to drip-dry on a cooling rack.

Zuccotto di Firenze
Florentine Zuccotto Frozen Dessert

📷

1 sponge cake (Pan di Spagna, see recipe B), Vin Santo or Marsala wine.

<u>Chocolate cream</u>: *1/4 cup butter, 1 teaspoon flour, 1/4 cup un-sweetened dark cocoa powder, 1/4 cup sugar, 1 cup milk, 31/2 oz. dark chocolate, chopped to small pieces.*

<u>White cream</u>: *2 cups whipping cream, 3/4 mixed chopped candied fruit, 1/4 cup powdered sugar.*

You'll need a mold shaped like a cap – 'Zuccotto'. Prepare the Sponge Cake and when cold slice it into rectangular strips – not too thick. Wet the strips with the Vin Santo and line the mold. Put it in the fridge. Prepare the chocolate cream: melt the butter and add the flour and cocoa powder. Whisk in the sugar and milk and cook, whisking continuously, over a low flame until thickened. When cooled put in fridge. Whip the cream with the powdered sugar until it forms stiff peaks. Divide it into two bowls. In one add the chopped candied fruit, delicately so that the cream remains thick. Take the second bowl of whipped cream and fold in the

cold chocolate cream and the chopped dark chocolate. Remove the mold from the fridge and pour in first the chocolate cream, then the white cream. Tap the mold gently on the counter to assure that the cream fills all of the empty spaces. Cover the top with Sponge Cake that has been dipped in Vin Santo. Place the 'Zuccotto' in the coldest section of the refrigerator for several hours before unmolding onto a serving platter. Remember: this dessert should be served as a 'semifreddo' (mousse) and not as an ice-cream cake that has been frozen. In the Florentine tradition 'Zuccotto' is the conclusion to any important dinner, such as Christmas.

ZUPPA ALL'INGLESE
FLORENTINE TRIFLE PUDDING

1 recipe sponge cake (Pan di Spagna, see recipe B).
FOR THE CREAM: 3 eggs, separated, 3/4 cup sugar, 3 tablespoons flour, 2 cups milk, boiled then cooled to room temperature.
FOR THE CHOCOLATE CREAM: 3 tablespoons butter, 1/4 cup dark un-sweetened cocoa powder, 3 tablespoons flour, 2 cups milk, boiled then cooled to room temperature, 3/4 cup sugar, 2 cups Vin Santo wine.

Prepare the sponge cake and set it aside to cool completely. Prepare the cream: beat the yolks with the sugar and flour. Whisk in the milk and place over a low flame. Cook, stirring continuously, until the surface begins to thicken. Boil for 2 minutes. Set aside to cool. Prepare the chocolate: mix the cocoa powder and flour together. Melt the butter in a small saucepan and whisk in the cocoa then the milk and finally the sugar. Cook over a low flame, stirring constantly, until

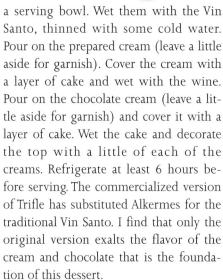

thickened, about 10 minutes. Set aside to cool. Slice the Sponge Cake into thin slices and place them in the bottom of a serving bowl. Wet them with the Vin Santo, thinned with some cold water. Pour on the prepared cream (leave a little aside for garnish). Cover the cream with a layer of cake and wet with the wine. Pour on the chocolate cream (leave a little aside for garnish) and cover it with a layer of cake. Wet the cake and decorate the top with a little of each of the creams. Refrigerate at least 6 hours before serving. The commercialized version of Trifle has substituted Alkermes for the traditional Vin Santo. I find that only the original version exalts the flavor of the cream and chocolate that is the foundation of this dessert.

ZUPPA OR PANE DOLCE DELLA PUERPERA
NEW MOTHER'S PUDDING

◆

4 slices day-old Italian bread, 2 cups red wine, 1 cup water, 4 tablespoons sugar.

Put the bread slices in a large bowl. Bring the wine and water to a boil and dip the bread in it. Sprinkle the slices with sugar. This isn't really a dessert but more an example of how ingeniously ingredients were put together to form a 'tutt'uno', or rather an all-in-one energetic yet very simple snack that is really quite delicious. This pudding was served especially to new mothers, since it was said to help produce more milk!

ZUPPA DI VISCIOLE
WILD CHERRY UDDING

◆

2.2 lbs very ripe wild cherries (or similar type cherries), 1 cup sugar, 1 teaspoon cinnamon, 1 recipe sponge cake (Pan di Spagna, see recipe B), 1/3 cup Rose liqueur (Rosolio di rose).

Pit the cherries and cook them with a little water, the sugar and cinnamon. Cool. Cut the prepared sponge cake into 3 layers and slice the layers into finger-sized strips. Place a layer of the strips in the bottom of a pan. Brush the cake with the rose liqueur and put some of the cherries and their liquid on top. Cover with another layer of cake and continue layering until the pan is filled. Cover and refrigerate several hours before serving. Turn the pudding out onto a serving dish and garnish with fresh rose buds... an elegant and unusual touch for a simple dessert. I find this dessert perfectly appropriate for a child's First Communion party. May: the month of cherries, roses and... Holy Communion!

ZUPPA TARTARA
RICOTTA AND APRICOT PUDDING

📷

1 1/3 cups fresh ricotta cheese, 1/2 cup milk, 1/2 cup powdered sugar, about 20-30 Ladyfinger cookies, 2 cups sweet Marsala, 1 cup apricot jam, apricots for garnish.
A VARIATION: 1/4 cup dark unsweetened cocoa powder, 1/4 cup sugar, 1 cup ricotta.

Mix the ricotta, milk and powdered sugar together with a wooden spoon. Dip the ladyfingers in the Marsala, squeeze them

gently, and place them in a loaf pan. Spread the cookies with apricot jam and some of the ricotta cream. Place another layer of cookies, apricot jam, cream. Continue until the loaf pan is filled. Put it in the refrigerator for 3 hours before serving. Turn out on serving platter but wait a few moments before removing the form to allow the pudding to drop down. Garnish with fresh apricot halves. Variation: Instead of apricot jam, make a mixture of cocoa powder, sugar and about 1 cup of ricotta. Alternate the layers using first the white then the dark ricotta mixtures.

ZUPPA VALDIMONTONE
OR "LA MONTONAIOLA"
VALDIMONTONE TRIFLE

◆

1 CAKE "TORTA 'LA BIANCA' DI PRATO" (see recipe): Alkermes liqueur, powdered sugar.
BOCCA DI DAMA (see recipe): 1/4 cup butter, 5 eggs, separated, 2/3 cup sugar, 1/2 cup flour, 1/4 cup potato flour, 1/4 teaspoon vanilla extract, pinch of salt.

First prepare the Torta "La Bianca" di Prato cake. Cool completely. Prepare the Bocca di Dama. Melt the butter and set aside to cool. Beat the egg yolks with the sugar until smooth and light. Beat the egg whites to stiff peaks and fold them into the prepared yolks. Sift the flour, potato flour and salt together and fold them into the eggs. Fold in the vanilla and cooled melted butter. Pour the batter into a buttered and floured 8" round cake pan and bake in a 190°C/375°F pre-heated oven for 40 minutes. The cake is cooked when it has doubled in volume. Cool completely.

Once both cakes are ready put them together. Slice them both into thin strips. Put one layer of "Torta 'La Bianca' di Prato" on the bottom of a serving bowl. Put a layer of Bocca di dama slices, that have been dipped in Alkermes, on top... alternate the layers until you reach the top of the bowl. End with the "Torta 'La Bianca' di Prato" on top and dust with powdered sugar.

BASIC RECIPES

A
CREMA PASTICCIERA
PASTRY CREAM
◆

1/2 cup sugar, 4 egg yolks, 1/3 cup corn starch, 2 cups milk, at room temperature, 1 teaspoon vanilla extract.

Whisk the yolks and sugar together - make sure that they don't thicken. Add the cornstarch and mix thoroughly. Pour the mixture into a saucepan and whisk in the milk and the vanilla. Stirring constantly, cook over a low flame for 2 minutes until thickened.
Cool before using. You can also flavor the cream with 3 tablespoons of either Vin Santo or Maraschino.

B
PAN DI SPAGNA
SPONGE CAKE
◆

6 eggs, separated, 1 teaspoon vanilla extract, grated rind of 1/2 lemon, 1 cup sugar, 1/2 cup flour, 1/3 cup potato flour, 3 tablespoons softened butter.

Beat the egg yolks until pale and thick, gradually adding the vanilla, sugar and lemon rind - mix well. Beat the egg whites until they are stiff. Fold the yolks and whites together making sure to fold from the bottom up. Mix the flour and the potato

flour together and slowly, slowly fold them into the egg mixture. Fold in from the bottom to the top. Butter and flour an 8" round baking pan and gently pour in the batter and bake in a pre-heated 190°C/375°F oven for about 30 minutes. Remove from pan and let cool completely before slicing. Sponge cake is versatile and can be the base for fruit, cream or chocolate desserts.
For birthdays, you can prepare three different sizes and layer them so that they form a pyramid that is pleasing to the eye. I suggest that you fill the layers with apricot jam and frost with a chocolate cream and candied cherries.

C
PASTA DI PANE
BREAD DOUGH
◆

16 oz. flour (00 type), 1 oz. active dry beer yeast, 1 cup tepid water, salt, optional: 1 tablespoon olive oil.

Dissolve the yeast in the tepid water and set aside. Mound the flour on a flat work surface and form a crater in the center. Add the salt and slowly pour in the prepared yeast. Start kneading, adding more and water as you go, until all of the yeast has been incorporated. You can also add the olive oil if you desire at this point.

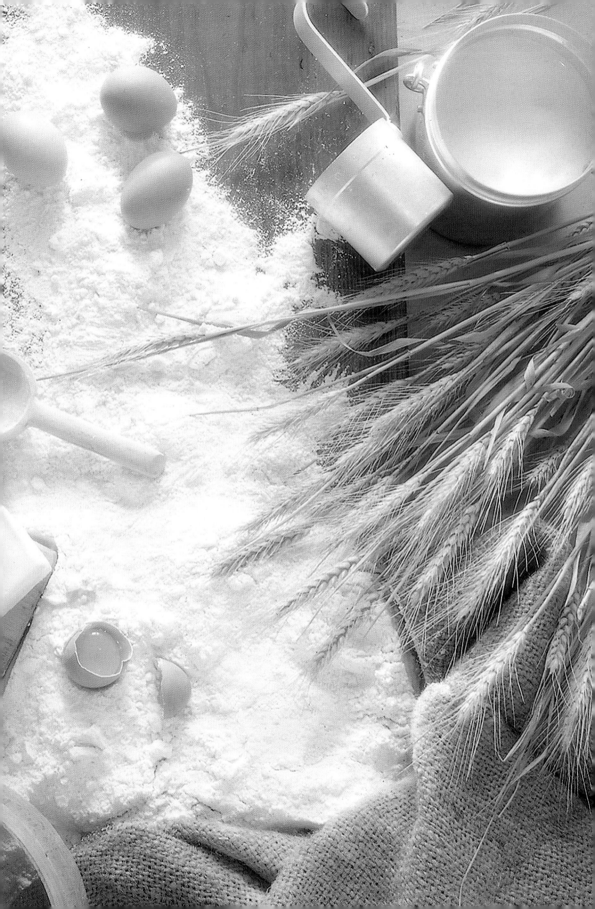

Knead the dough for 10 minutes or until it is smooth and elastic. Put it in a bowl to rise, covered with a cloth and put in a dry place. When the dough has doubled in bulk, punch it down and proceed with any recipe that requires simple bread dough.

D
PASTA FROLLA
PASTRY DOUGH

◆

11/2 cups flour, 1/2 teaspoon salt, 1 egg + 1 yolk, 3/4 cup sugar, grated rind 1 lemon, 3/4 cup softened butter.

Form a mound with the flour and salt on a flat work surface. Break the egg and yolk into the center and add the sugar and grated rind. Blend gently with your hands. Add the butter, in small pieces, to the flour and knead quickly into a ball. Cover with plastic wrap and refrigerate for at least 45 minutes before using.

In Tuscany we tend to substitute butter with olive oil. In this case, you'd need 1 cup of oil.

E
PASTA PER PICCOLI DOLCI
TARTLET DOUGH

◆

1 cup flour, 1/2 cup + 2 tablespoons butter, 3 tablespoons sugar, pinch of salt, water — about 7 tablespoons.

Knead the flour and softened butter, salt and sugar on a flat surface with your hands. Working slowly, break-up the butter until it is 'pea' sized. Add cold water, a little at a time, and knead until the dough is smooth and elastic. Form a ball, cover with plastic wrap and set it in the fridge for at least 2 hours.

Roll out the dough on a floured surface – use additional flour to prevent sticking. Fill any-size small tartlet shapes.

Line the prepared tartlets with some dried beans (to prevent bubbles) and bake them in a pre-heated 190°C/375°F oven for 20 minutes.

Once golden, remove from oven and discard the beans.

Fill the cooled tartlets with whatever you like: mousse, creams, etc.

F
PASTA SFOGLIA
FLAKY PASTRY DOUGH

◆

1 lb. flour, 1 lb. slightly softened butter, pinch of salt.

Divide the flour in two parts: one that is 2/3 of the quantity and one that is 1/3. Place the larger half on a flat surface and add the salt and 1/2 cup cold water. Begin kneading. Add, a little at a time, another 1/2 cup of water. Knead until solid and smooth. Form a rectangle shape. Flatten the top and cut a large 'x' onto the surface using a sharp knife. Wrap in plastic and set in the fridge for 30 minutes. Knead the remaining dough with all of the butter. Work very quickly so that the butter doesn't melt. Form a rectangle shape, wrap it in plastic wrap and set it in the fridge. Remove the loaves from the refrigerator and roll out the 'x' loaf, forming a large 16 x 16" square. Place the 'butter' loaf in the center, fold the top and bottom of the rolled-out square over the top, leaving the sides of the square open. Flatten with the rolling pin so that the 'butter loaf' evenly fills the center.

By now you should have an almost 2-inch high rectangle. Fold the two open sides of the rectangle towards the center so that they meet but don't overlap. Fold in half the entire rectangle, wrap it in plastic and put it in the fridge for 1 hour. Remove the pastry from the refrigerator and roll it out in the same manner as before: make a square, fold it over, flatten it, fold-over the open edges towards the center and then fold in half. Wrap in plastic and set in the fridge

again for 1 hour.

Carry out this process four more times: it is necessary to repeat this process a total of 6 times so that the butter fat is distributed evenly within the layers of dough and assumes it's classic flakiness.

G
TORTA RUSTICA DEI SETTE CUCCHIAI
SEVEN SPOON RUSTIC CAKE

♦

2 1/2 cups flour, 3 teaspoons baking powder, 7 tablespoons each: olive oil, sugar, milk, grated rind 1 lemon, butter.

Mix the flour and baking powder together in a large bowl. Stirring with a wooden spoon, add the milk and sugar. Mix well.

Add the olive oil and mix vigorously until the batter is smooth. Sprinkle the grated rind on top and set aside for 10 minutes. Butter and flour an 8" round pan and pour in the batter.

Bake for 40 minutes in a pre-heated 190°C/ 375°F oven.

Test with a toothpick for doneness. Cool before serving. This cake is very versatile and can be served in many ways and for many occasions.

Filled with homemade jam (like apricot) and sprinkled with some cold milk it is a perfect afternoon snack.

For a delicious birthday cake, fill it with chocolate cream, wet with a little liqueur and cover the cake with freshly whipped cream.

CONTENTS

C O N T E N T S

RECIPES

BASIC RECIPES